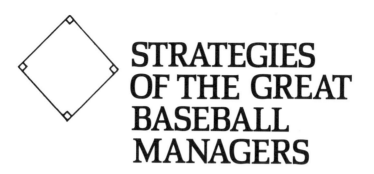

STRATEGIES
OF THE GREAT
BASEBALL
MANAGERS

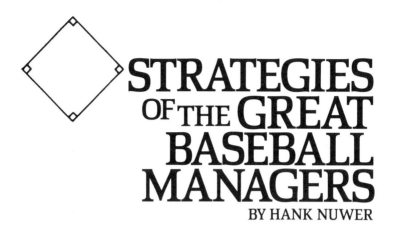

STRATEGIES OF THE GREAT BASEBALL MANAGERS
BY HANK NUWER

Franklin Watts
New York/London/Toronto/Sydney/1988

Photographs courtesy of: National Baseball Library,
Cooperstown, N.Y.: 67 (top), 68 (top), 69, 71, 72 (bottom);
Bettman/UPI Newsphotos: pp. 67 (bottom), 68 (bottom),
70 (bottom), 72 (top); AP/Wide World Photos: p. 70 (top).

Library of Congress Cataloging-in-Publication Data

Nuwer, Hank.
Strategies of the great baseball managers / by Hank Nuwer.
p. cm.
Bibliography: p.
Summary: Examines the careers of prominent baseball managers who
stamped their methods and personalities on the game, including
Connie Mack, Casey Stengel, and Sparky Anderson.
Includes index.
ISBN 0-531-10601-2
1. Baseball—United States—Managers—Biography—Juvenile
literature. [1. Baseball—Managers.] I. Title.
GV865.A1N87 1988
796.357′092′2—dc19
[B]
[920]   88-5739 CIP AC

Especially for Jenine and my sons, Chris and Adam; but also for Steve Bania and Fraser Drew who helped the author go right, when everyone else predicted he'd go wrong. And in memory of my beloved dad who learned to swing a mean fungo in his forties because he knew there was no better way to reach his baseball-mad boy.

CONTENTS

INTRODUCTION
11

One
CAP ANSON:
THE GRAND OLD MAN OF BASEBALL
14

Two
CONNIE MACK:
MR. BASEBALL
24

Three
FRANK CHANCE:
THE PEERLESS LEADER
36

Four
JOHN JOSEPH MCGRAW:
THE LITTLE NAPOLEON
46

Five
MILLER HUGGINS:
THE MIGHTY MITE
57

Six
JOE MCCARTHY:
THE PUSHBUTTON MANAGER
73

Seven
CASEY STENGEL:
THE OLD PROFESSOR
84

Eight
LEO DUROCHER:
FURY ON THE FIELD
96

Nine
WALT ALSTON:
MANAGING YEAR-BY-YEAR
106

Ten
EARL WEAVER:
LORD BALTIMORE
116

Eleven
SPARKY ANDERSON:
FROM CAR SALESMAN TO LEGEND
126

Twelve
WHITEY HERZOG:
THE MAN WHO PAID HIS DUES
135

NOTES 145   SOURCES 151   INDEX 155

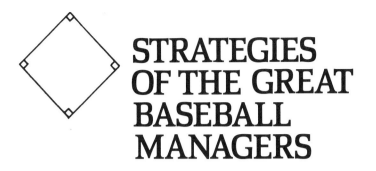

STRATEGIES OF THE GREAT BASEBALL MANAGERS

INTRODUCTION

Baseball has always played musical chairs with its managers, and in recent years so many pilots have been fired so quickly, that the average tenure is now only two years. Keeping track of new baseball managers is like keeping track of entertainers at Las Vegas hotels. They come, they go. For example, although Earl Weaver was with Baltimore from 1968 to 1982 (before his unfortunate comeback), the Oakland A's and New York Yankees changed managers ten times, the Texas Rangers-cum-Washington Senators twelve times.

Yesterday's managers had a difficult time, but a John McGraw never had to face the problems that today's managers must conquer. Free agency, extended holdouts, drug abuse, and unending contract squabbles are just part of the unwanted baggage a manager carries around when he signs a contract. Even the 1927 Yankees might not have won if Babe Ruth, Lou Gehrig, and Waite Hoyt had been allowed to opt for free agency. Team depth is no longer desirable. Just look at the dissension that tore apart a fine young Cincinnati team in 1987 when manager Pete Rose platooned his stars. And when a team does win a division title, the next year its opponents are giving pitchers an extra day's rest to knock the king off the top of the hill.

Moreover, the mobility of managers makes the task of establishing an all-time record a difficult one. Ask a friend to name the twelve best football coaches, and no doubt you will find yourself in an argument. So many great college and professional coaches have evolved over the years that no two lists can ever agree.

The same cannot be said of baseball. Try to come up with a list of the dozen all-time managers, and you begin to falter after the first half-dozen. Few managers have dominated their respective eras the way Casey Stengel did during the fifties or Joe McCarthy did from 1936 to 1943—both, of course, accomplished great things with the New York Yankees. What further complicates the issue is that many great tacticians—most notably Gene Mauch—have failed to appear in a single World Series.

Nonetheless, *Strategies of the Great Baseball Managers* attempts to honor twelve men whom the author regards as the all-time best at their jobs. These are men who not only commanded respect from their players as master strategists, but who also succeeded in winning world championships. Men such as Walter Alston, Leo Durocher, and Sparky Anderson have seen the game change many times during their tenures, but they've been wily and wise enough to adapt when they've had to do so.

This book also pays homage to Connie Mack and John McGraw, who stayed in baseball longer than was good for them or their later teams but who proved themselves to be winners and did more than any other duo to make the game respectable, overcoming its image as a sport of gamblers and drunkards.

Some prominent names are missing from this book. Any list of great sports personalities is, of course, subjective, but the author has established certain criteria which have eliminated some otherwise notable managers.

One requirement was longevity. All managers included in this book had to demonstrate their managerial skills over the course of ten years or more. This criterion eliminated Dick Howser, the great manager of the Kansas City Royals and New York Yankees, who died well before his time in 1987 of a brain tumor.

However, mere longevity was not enough for automatic inclusion. A manager had to establish himself as a winner over the long haul, thus striking the colorful Brooklyn manager Wilbert Robinson from the book, since Robbie's two pennants in his distinguished nineteen-year career were not enough to overcome the stigma of his thirteen second-division finishes. Likewise, Detroit manager Hughie Jennings finished first his initial three seasons as a manager, then never won another pennant again in his fourteen-year career; Bucky Harris won two pennants his first two seasons and then survived twelve straight so-so campaigns. Another factor in selecting coaches was their post-season record, eliminating not only fine tacticians such as Gene Mauch but also Chuck Dressen, whose World Series winning percentage is a shabby .385.

The most difficult choices were among contemporary managers, and it was difficult to omit both Billy Martin and the equally well traveled Dick Williams. Their many fans may quarrel with their exclusion, but suffice it to say that if this book celebrated the *fifteen* best managers, both would have qualified.

The author hopes that this book helps the reader gain some perspective on how these dozen great managers helped the national pastime become, in the words of Curt Smith, author of *Voices of the Game*, "the only sport you can truly love." No other sport is so much fun to second-guess. No other field generals are so loved or hated as baseball managers. Although it is true that baseball managers were hired to be fired, some of them were also hired to be admired. This book celebrates the best and most successful strategists of all time. Enjoy!

1 CAP ANSON: THE GRAND OLD MAN OF BASEBALL

Adrian Constantine (Cap) Anson's Hall of Fame plaque in Cooperstown says that he was the "greatest hitter and greatest National League player-manager of [the] 19th Century." As a manager, he led his Chicago White Stockings to five pennants. As a player, he batted .300 or better for twenty years, capturing four batting championships. Anson commanded respect from his men and fans alike. He was the first ballplayer to be regarded as a national hero. Managing in an era when rival skippers used mainly luck to win them games, he recognized that games could also be won by improved hitting, defense, and baserunning. Moreover, while molding his Chicago White Stockings of the mid-1880s into the best team in the National League, the non-drinking Anson set a public example for clean living at a time when the public considered ballplayers to be drunks and gamblers.

Anson was descended from English and Irish forebears who came to America in the seventeenth century. His parents were originally from the pretty Michigan towns of Adrian and Constantine but settled in Marshalltown, Iowa, which then was Potawatomi Indian country. Perhaps homesick for their hometowns, they named their son Adrian Constantine. Born on April 17, 1852, like Abe Lincoln in a log cabin, he was the first white baby born in Marshalltown.

Anson had little choice but to grow up a fanatic sports enthusiast. With little to do on the prairie but read and compete in games of speed, skill, and strength, the boy was fortunate to be both athletically and intellectually gifted. His only drawback was that he was never fleet of foot, losing footraces to swifter Indian opponents. In 1866, Anson's father started a topnotch Marshalltown baseball team that barnstormed against some of the best teams in the Midwest. The roster was made up mainly of the Anson clan, including fourteen-year-old Adrian, his father, and one brother.

Young Anson's first memorable game occurred in 1868, when his Marshalltown team played the then-amateur Forest City Club. This Rockford, Illinois-based team played a tough schedule, including games against the Cincinnati Red Stockings, baseball's first professional team. Forest City's Albert Spalding, destined to become a 262-game-winning pitcher, observed that Adrian Anson was the best player on the Marshalltown roster.

Unable to attract a pro offer, however, Anson enrolled at Notre Dame University, where he persuaded the Catholic institution to establish varsity baseball. The infielder served as team captain until Forest City—on Spalding's recommendation—offered Anson $65 per month to play for its newly franchised National Association of Baseball Players Club in 1871. Given the chance to turn professional, the college boy abandoned his books in favor of baseball. In 1872, the underfinanced River City's franchise folded, but Anson convinced the Philadelphia Athletics, also of the National Association, to sign him for $1,250 a season.[1] The baby-faced player teammates called the "Marshalltown Infant" starred for four years in the City of Brotherly Love.

But in 1875, Boston newspapers reported that the Chicago White Stockings were about to stage player raids on their opponents. William Hulbert, a Windy City booster who claimed he'd "rather be a lamp post in Chicago than a millionaire anywhere else," had persuaded Boston's pitching ace "Al" Spalding to become the player-manager of the Chicago team for the then-unheard of sum of $4,000. Hulbert had a grandiose scheme to start a rival association, the National League of Professional Baseball Clubs, which hoped to rid the sport of the drunkards and gamblers that had sullied the so-called national game. Spalding, a cagey businessman who later made a fortune in sporting goods, began raiding National Association clubs to acquire talented players, including Anson of the Athletics to play third. "The champion nine should have champion salaries," Spalding promised Anson and the other defectors.[2]

But during the winter of 1875, Anson suffered misgivings about his decision "to secede" as the post-Civil War newspapers called his defection. His new love was a Philadelphian who wanted her future husband to remain at home. Anson begged Hulbert and his friend Spalding to let him out of the arrangement, even offering to buy his own release for $1,000, then threatening to break the contract when the two refused his offer. "You have his contract; he has promised me," Spalding told his boss. "He'll play with Chicago."[3]

Spalding, it turned out, was right. The Philadelphian decided he could not go back on his word to Chicago. When the White Stockings' spring practice opened, Adrian Anson—a lifelong dandy—showed up in a Prince Albert coat and striped trousers to look over his new teammates. He had come to argue one last time, but perhaps upon seeing the talent of the men Spalding had assembled, he suddenly changed his mind.

"Toss me one, Al?" he asked the manager.

"What? With those togs on?" came the rebuke.

Off came Anson's frock coat. Spalding fired the ball to him. "Now Anse, come tomorrow in uniform," said the grinning Spalding, who had no way of knowing that the youngster in striped pants was destined to play in Chicago for twenty-three years.[4]

Chicago was an exciting place to be in 1876. A great fire had occurred five years earlier, but the undaunted inhabitants had built an even greater, more exciting city in its place. In a few years the sprawling city would cover 181 square miles, making it at that time the largest urban center in the nation. Skyscrapers first appeared in Chicago, and the metropolis became a leader in the arts, industry, and education. Yet underneath all this prosperity, Chicagoans couldn't help but feel inferior to the more established centers of civilization in Boston and New York. Consequently, when a genuine hero of the sporting world such as Adrian Anson appeared in town, the citizens worshipped him as a young god.

The excitement of having a professional baseball team in town was evident in early sports stories published in the *Chicago Tribune*. An unbylined *Tribune* account of Chicago's visit to Louisville, Kentucky, to play its first professional game, showed clear bias in favor of the White Stockings, who won 4–0 despite collecting only eight hits. "People in Chicago who believe that they have the strongest batting team in the league will look at the above score with doubt on that point when they see the best men without credit for even a single hit. It should be explained that the ball was the deadest possible to be found, and with it long hits were impossible. Then, again, the ground was soggy, and the ball could not be hit hard enough to bound."

Anson, in that first game, collected his first hit in a Chicago uniform. The *Tribune* added that the third baseman "faced some stiff hits and fielded them in beautiful style." In addition, his throws to first were "accurate as rifle shooting." The season went as smoothly for the White

Stockings as that first game, resulting in a first-place finish for Chicago and a .348 batting average for Anson.

Fans had little trouble distinguishing Anson from the other players that year. In the first place, the baby-faced Anson was the only starter without facial hair that season; he hadn't yet begun growing his own trademark handlebar mustache. Secondly, that year Spalding dressed his players like jockeys, in caps of different colors, to promote his sporting goods business. And when that business began to take up all of his free time, particularly after he won a contract to supply the National League with all its base-balls, Spalding retired from the game as a player-manager in 1879. His last bit of business was to recommend that Hulbert name Anson as his replacement.

From the first day on the job, Anson took his duties seriously, although he preferred to be called Captain or "Cap" rather than manager. When his friend Spalding (who was to become White Sox president in 1884 after Hulbert's death) stepped onto the field one day to second-guess a decision, the new manager drove him away with a volley of threats and oaths.

Anson's first bit of managerial strategy was to revamp the aging club of veterans who had played for Spalding, keeping only himself in the lineup. He put himself at first base, trading a popular player named Joe Start to Providence. The trade demonstrated to fans that Anson was willing to make difficult, even unpopular, decisions. Thirty-four-year-old Start, whose nickname was "Old Reliable," was a good athlete. A career .300 hitter who played until he was forty-four, Start's departure convinced Chicago players and fans that every ballplayer was expendable, save Anson.

The move to first no doubt prolonged Anson's career, but he received some criticism for dumping the smooth-fielding Start. Anson's slow footedness around the initial sack made him a liability. He once committed fifty-eight errors in a single season at first base. However, his splendid hitting more than compensated for his weak glove. He truly came into his own as a hitter after he became a big-league manager, becoming the first man to hit .400 or better in 1879, hitting .407 to win the first of his four batting titles.

It took only one year for Anson to build a championship team. Anson's troops finished third in 1879 behind second-place Boston and the pennant-winning Providence Grays, who were managed by George Wright, the only man to finish first in his only year as a big-league skipper. Ironically, one of the most valuable players for Providence that season was former Chicagoan Joe Start.

But in 1880, the White Stockings under Anson evolved into one of the game's great dynasties, winning five pennants in seven seasons. The 1880 team had a 67–17 season for a record .798 winning percentage. Despite the liability Anson himself was as a fielder, the rest of the team's defense was so strong that the press heralded it as the "Stonewall infield." During the pennant-winning 1880 season, Anson conceived of the idea of rotating two pitchers and using one of his reserve players to mop up in relief. Before this, managers mostly used one pitcher for the bulk of an eighty-four-game season, simply releasing a hurler after he inevitably threw out his arm, just as Al Spalding had begun to do when he retired. The Chicago mound duo of Larry Corcoran and Fred Goldsmith, over a three-year period, won 178 out of 252 games.

Without question the 6'2", 220-pound Anson inspired his Chicago team to give its best efforts. According to baseball historian Arthur Bartlett, Anson was the first great baseball field general. "Earnest, fearless, single-minded and forthright to a fault, he was always out to win, and he ran the team with an iron hand to that end," wrote Bartlett. "His arguments with umpires were famous, often ending in a comprehensive summary of his views directed not only at the umpire but at the opposing team and the grandstand, too. The cranks loved it, and though Anson himself was not exactly the lovable type, their veneration for him bordered on worship."[5]

The teetotaling father of four managed to get more out of his players by demanding that they appear on the field in reasonable physical shape, although few players had his muscular build. Once, to ensure that his players started the season in shape, Anson took them to Hot Springs, Arkansas, to sweat out a winter's accumulation of alcohol. Because of this, historians have credited the Chicago manager with beginning the practice of spring training.

The manager was adept at assessing talent back in a time when teams failed to employ scouts. During the 1880s, Chicago stars included such talented players as base-stealing superstar Mike "King" Kelly, pitcher Fred Goldsmith (who won twenty or more games in four consecutive years), and speedster Billy Sunday.

Anson himself discovered Sunday on a trip back to his native Marshalltown in 1883, when the youth—then a hearse driver—won a carnival race, and the manager vowed he would make a ballplayer out of him. He kept his faith in Sunday even after the youth struck out the first thirteen times he came to the plate and the *Boston Globe* gave this "pet of Anson's" a grade of zero. However, Sunday improved and became Chicago's top reserve and was reputed to be the fastest man in the league, stealing up to ninety-six bases in a single season.

In those years Chicago possessed not only speed but power. Despite playing in a so-called "dead-ball" era, Anson's 1884 White Stockings—known as the "Heroic Legion of Baseball"—belted 140 home runs, a record that remained until the 1927 New York Yankees surpassed it. Because his teams were so adept at hitting the long ball, Anson disdained the practice of bunting, but he was one of the first to rely on the hit-and-run and running game. The team was led by Ed Williamson's twenty-seven home runs, whose accomplishment remained until Babe Ruth broke it thirty-five years later.

When strategy failed Anson, the manager used his fists and powerful voice to get results from his hard-drinking team. The Captain had to be in excellent physical shape to manhandle them. No less than seven members of the 1880s dynasty team stood six-foot or better, but Anson himself had no problem handling them over the course of his twenty-seven-year career. However, the overbearing size of Anson's swift-footed giants intimidated lesser teams wearing tight-fitting, sleeveless uniforms that Spalding had designed to show off their muscles. "It used to be a case of 'eat-'em-up, Jake,' " said outfielder-catcher King Kelly. "We had most of 'em whipped before we threw a ball; they were scared to death."

Even more so than Anson, Kelly was the darling of Chicago fans. Kelly was a fine runner on the base paths and thrilled fans with both hook slides and headfirst dives to steal as many as eighty-seven bases in a season. He also came up with ideas that Anson used as everyday strategic weapons, such as backing up the infield on throws when he was in the outfield and signaling the fielders what pitch was coming when he was behind the plate. An important part of Anson's strategy was simply to order his Chicagoans to play hard. In a must-game against Providence for the 1882 pennant, King Kelly's body-block slide into George Wright caused the infielder to drop the ball, leading to two runs and a Chicago victory.

However, even though Kelly led the National League in batting in 1886 with a .388 average (and a league-leading 155 runs scored) en route to the 1886 pennant, Anson concluded that his star's off-the-field drinking was detrimental to the good of the team. Thus, when Spalding approached his manager to ask him if he would sell Kelly to Boston for $10,000—then the highest price ever paid for a player—Anson readily agreed. "Sure, spare anybody," he grunted laconically.[6]

Anson dealt another star outfielder, George Gore, a career .303 hitter, because Gore had made what the manager considered unreasonable salary demands. He also sold speedster Billy Sunday to Pittsburgh and peddled future Hall-of-Famer John Clarkson to Boston. With fifty-three wins against only sixteen losses in 1885, Clarkson had led the White Stockings to win the pennant by two games over New York, then added thirty-five wins in 1886. Anson went sour on Clarkson because in an early version of the World Series in 1886, the star had thrown a wild pitch in the tenth inning of the final game to give the series to the St. Louis Browns of the American Association.

Anson's conviction that he could win with any nine men as long as he was one of them turned out to be his undoing. He never won another pennant, although he did lead Chicago (called Anson's young "Colts" in later years) to three second-place finishes before being forced out of Chicago in 1897. One of his greatest achievements occurred in 1889, when the newly formed Brotherhood League raided his team of seven starters and, despite a ragtag collection of minor leaguers and sandlot players, his team finished second, with Anson singlehandedly leading the team with a .342 batting average. In his book, *Baseball's Greatest Managers* (1985), author Harvey Frommer attributed Anson's success in 1889 to " 'Inside baseball'—coordination of infield and outfield play, cautious baserunning, and scientific, though by today's standards, basic approach—[which] marked his managing technique that season."

In February 1898, James Hart—Spalding's successor as Chicago president who had dourly predicted that under Anson Chicago might win a pennant sometime in the next 1,500 years—relieved the manager of his duties. Newspapers stopped referring to the team as the Colts, and a few mournfully dubbed it the "Orphans." As if to break from the old White Stocking heritage, Hart then spitefully changed the team's hosiery to navy blue stockings.

Seen in retrospect, there was one lone black mark on Anson's career, but it was a damaging one indeed. In 1887 Anson led the battle against allowing the New York Giants to sign a black player named George Stovey. The manager's hatred of blacks contributed to a shameful color barrier that was to exist for more than fifty years in the major leagues. Anson even kept a black mascot on the team named Clarence Duval so that his superstitious Chicagoans could run their fingers through the youth's hair for good luck. In 1888, he bitterly fought a movement on the part of several owners that would have allowed black players to compete in the major leagues. Not only were twenty-five black men in the minor leagues banished forever, so were Oberlin-educated Moses Fleetwood Walker and his brother Welday who played in the majors. "After Cap Anson drew the color line," said Daniel Okrent and Harris Lewine, editors of *The Ultimate Baseball Book*, "Welday wrote the President of the Tri-State League, George McDermott: 'The rule that you have passed is a public disgrace.' "

But aside from this, Anson's twenty-year career (he managed twenty-two games for the Giants in 1898) as a manager was impressive. His teams won 1,297 games against only 957 losses for a .575 winning percentage. Similarly, "Pop" Anson—as his players called him in the 1890s—was arguably the greatest player of the nineteenth century, batting .303 at age forty-six, and ending his career with 3,022 hits for a .333 career average.

The end of his life was far from idyllic, however. In his older years he toured in Vaudeville with his daughters to earn money, allowing fans to throw him simulated baseballs that he batted off the stage. He died on April 14, 1922, and was accorded a hero's wake by the citizens of Chicago.

2 ◇ CONNIE MACK: MR. BASEBALL

During the fifty-one years that Connie Mack managed the AL's Philadelphia franchise, he maintained an uncanny ability for anticipating where an opposing batsman would hit the ball. Mack repositioned his defense by waving his scorecard until the fielders stood just where the manager wanted them to stand. One day he pointed his scorecard like a conductor's baton, moving outfielder Charlie Metro eight or ten steps to one side, then back a bit, then another step to the side. Sure enough, the batter hit a scorching shot right at Metro's chest. The fielder snagged it for the third out of the inning and trotted into the dugout.

"You know what I think?" Metro said to a fellow player while shaking his head in wonder. "I think that Mr. Mack is the best outfielder in the American League."[1]

Even the veteran Ty Cobb followed Mack's advice when the manager ordered him to shift. Cobb, who closed his career with the Athletics, grumbled under his breath but moved nonetheless. Sure enough, a line drive came his way, and he could have caught the liner sitting in an easy chair. "I've heard a lot about your scorecard," the normally phlegmatic Cobb said to Mack. "From now on, I'm going to believe in it."[2]

Cobb was only one of many topnotch baseball men who admired Connie Mack. Jimmy Dykes, a longtime player for Mack and the manager's choice to succeed him as Athletics' manager, called him "one of the greatest managers who ever lived." The great Yankee manager Miller Huggins patterned his own career after him, and former Yankee pitcher Bob Shawkey—who played for both Mack and Huggins—said that the Philadelphia manager was the best he ever played under.

In his fifty-one years managing the same team—a record for longevity that probably will never be broken—Mack won nine pennants and five World Series, establishing himself as one of the finest baseball minds of all time. The holder of the big-league record for most games won by a manager (3,776), he not only kept up with the game's changes but instigated many himself. "I have never known a day when I didn't learn something new about this game," he liked to tell reporters.[3]

Cornelius Alexander McGillicuddy (he shortened it to Connie Mack after signing a baseball contract) was born during the Civil War, in East Brookfield, Massachusetts, then a town of just three hundred inhabitants, on December 22, 1862. Curiously, until he was seventy-five, he celebrated his birthday on December 23. But in his old age he discovered he'd been born a day earlier than he thought he had been.

Young Connie hardly knew his father. Michael McGillicuddy, an Irish immigrant, was away fighting for the Union in the Civil War when his wife Mary gave birth to Connie. Upon his return, Michael worked in a cotton mill, forcing his nine-year-old son to work there in summers for 35 cents a day as an errand boy and elevator operator. In Connie's early teens, Michael died, and at age sixteen, the boy quit school and took a job in the Green and Twitchell Shoe Factory, because, he said, "the business of feeding a sizable and hollow-legged Irish family [went] squarely on my hatrack shoulders." But he had no intention of remaining in such a depressing existence. Despite his gaunt, 6′1″ build that earned him the nickname of Slats, he starred as a catcher on East Brookfield's top-rated town team, playing an exhibition game against Cap Anson's Chicago National Leaguers. His first earnings came from his share of what was inside a passed hat.

Late in life, Mack insisted that he always knew he would escape the poverty his parents had suffered. "The big thing about baseball is that if a fellow has the ability there's no limit to the heights to which he can rise," wrote the manager in *Connie Mack's Baseball Book*.

The youth's ability behind the plate was his ticket out of the shoe factory. The manager of the Meriden (Connecticut) minor league team discovered him and offered him a salary of $90 a month, less than he took home from the factory. But before accepting, he sought his mother's approval. Aware of the reputation that baseball players had for carousing and rowdy behavior, Mother McGillicuddy expressed her fears. "I won't ask you to make any promises," she told him, "but remember what I tell you now. You'll never get anywhere drinking and fighting."[4]

Baseball then was in its primitive stage. Only one umpire worked a game, and he was often attacked with fists as well as words. "Pop bottles flew like confetti," Mack said.[5]

When the gentlemanly Mack entered the game, he had to endure bench jockeying behind the plate because he wore a fingerless buckskin glove with a piece of raw steak concealed in the palm. Catchers who wore gloves were marked as sissies in those years.

The nineteenth-century version of the game of baseball bore little resemblance to its twentieth-century cousin. Catchers then stood well away from the pitcher to snare balls on the first hop. Pitchers stood 45 feet from the batter. For a while, batters were allowed seven balls and four strikes; during one year (1887), bases on balls were scored as hits. Batters ordered the opposing pitcher to throw the ball high or low, outside or inside.

Mack had difficulty adjusting to the rule changes regarding hitting. His average suffered after he could no longer ask hurlers to throw to his strength. He "couldn't hit for sour apples" after pitchers denied him the high balls he craved, winding up with a .251 career average. But he was always a reliable fielder and a solid handler of pitchers, although a bit of a rogue when it came to rules-bending. One of his favorite illegal tricks was to "tip" the bats of opposing hitters when they swung, causing them to swing late and with less power. "Why, I just help the hitters hit the ball, that's all," said Mack mischievously.[6]

Mack's early career was nomadic. He moved up from the minors on September 11, 1886, to Washington in the National League but proved a better fielder than hitter. From Washington he moved to Buffalo in 1890, playing catcher and the infield for the upstart (and soon extinct) Brotherhood League and investing his savings in the franchise. By then he had married Margaret Hogan, a girl from his hometown of East Brookfield, and had three children in succession, Earle, Roy, and Margaret. Needless to say, he was all but wiped out financially when the league folded, then suffered another heartache when Margaret, only twenty-six, suddenly died, and he had to leave his children with his mother. Pittsburgh of the National League picked him up, but his playing career was slowed in 1893 when he fractured his ankle in a game against Boston.

In 1894, he became the player-manager of the Pittsburgh franchise, suffering through three straight second-division finishes. But while at Pittsburgh, he showed that he had taken his mother's advice to heart, instituting a rule that forbade his players to imbibe alcohol. Throughout his career, he became a symbol of gentleness, never cursing his players except once in a blue moon behind closed doors, and never smoking.

After enduring three years in the minors as a manager from 1897 to 1900, Connie Mack's break came when he was offered the job of managing the Philadelphia Athletics in the newly formed American League and assuming partial ownership of the team. He wasn't troubled by the National League's derision of its rival. In fact, when Manager John McGraw chortled that "the American League's got a white elephant in Philadelphia," Mack defiantly called his team the White Elephants as a nickname and adopted the beast as its symbol.

"The Tall Tactician"—as Mack came to be known—made an immediate impact on the American League, finishing fourth in the team's first season and first in 1902, its second year. He demanded that his players participate in pregame skull sessions, going over strategy and opponents' tactics. Mack was the first to adopt this pregame ritual, and soon many disciples imitated the practice. "I am rather proud to say that I began the business of conducting [pregame] meetings," wrote Mack in an autobiographical article for *The Saturday Evening Post* in 1936. "There was only one unfortunate aftermath. The boys all began to ask me questions I couldn't answer."

As he matured, Mack's scouting reports became more complex, including those on his own players. After the 1930 season ended, the manager's statistics showed that leftfielder Al Simmons was his most valuable player in late innings, clouting fourteen home runs in the eighth or ninth inning that year. Today's managers take such information for granted, but in those days Mack's research was revolutionary. Before Mack came along, many otherwise astute baseball men said that luck played a major factor in whether a team won or lost, but the A's manager poohpoohed that notion. "There is no luck in Big League baseball," he insisted. "In a schedule of 154 games, the lucky and the unlucky plays break about even, except in the matter of injuries."[7]

In 1901, Mack began a continuing search for ideal "Mackmen"—smart players who didn't carouse. He wanted them because he believed them to be winners, and as a consequence, his cleancut stars helped baseball overcome its sullied image. The stiff collar, tie, and business suit he wore on the bench contrasted with the rumpled uniforms of tobacco-spitting rival managers.

That first player in the Mack mold was Eddie Plank, a twenty-five-year-old southpaw who had never played baseball until talked into it by a coach at tiny Gettysburg College in Pennsylvania. Mack preferred college-educated fellows, saying that they "put intelligence and scholarship into the game." With such players, the manager was content to rely on their instincts, seldom giving a pitcher or batter a direct order unless he clearly saw a better course of action.

Relying on a sizzling fastball and a curve that he threw at varying speeds, plus a slow deliberate style on the mound that caused irritated batters to lose their poise, Plank won seventeen games as a rookie in 1901. In 1902 he won twenty to help Mack win his first pennant.

But Mack also endured the presence of the game's daffiest oddballs, provided that they had talent. One thing that could be said about Mack was that he gave his people a chance to succeed or fail. The eccentric Rube Waddell, a pitcher whom the great Cy Young considered the best left-hander in the game, pitched six years for Mack, averaging twenty-two victories and more than 200 strikeouts a season (including 349 strikeouts in 1904). Nothing was too wild for Waddell's lively spirit, whether it be wrestling alligators, throwing the baton in parades, riding fire engines at breakneck speed, or disappearing for days to go fishing. He'd been judged too wild a drinker to control by Pittsburgh manager Fred Clarke and was languishing in the minors when Connie Mack sent two Pinkerton detectives to fetch him from Los Angeles (then in the Pacific Coast League) in 1902. Waddell responded immediately, winning twenty-four and losing only seven games that pennant-winning season, striking out 210 batters. There was a brief uproar when the pitcher tried to drown himself because a woman he was in love with rejected him, but a teammate saved him.

Because he considered Waddell talented, the manager tolerated the pitcher's excesses, even when the player audaciously called his boss by his first name, scandalizing the other players who always referred to him as "Mr. Mack." In 1902, Mack gave professional football a one-year fling, coaching the National Football League's Philadelphia Athletics and employing the 6'2", 196-pound Waddell as a player on the gridiron.

In 1905 even Mack's patience with Waddell ran out. The pitcher had a 26–11 record going into the last month of the season, when he injured his arm in a horseplay scuffle with fellow pitcher Andy Coakley, a twenty-game winner that year. Waddell was unable to play against John McGraw's Giants in the World Series, and Mack blamed his absence for the A's eventual defeat, trading his zany future Hall-of-Famer two years later. "I just couldn't stand him any longer," admitted the exasperated manager.[8]

With the exception of Waddell, Mack was revered by his players, although he kept his distance from them. One rule that he imposed upon himself was never to dress with the players after a game, allowing him a full day to cool off before speaking to them after a loss. This allowed him to look at the game in perspective. He might still bawl out his men for making bonehead plays, but he could do so without losing his temper. "You never saw him after a game," recalled Bob Shawkey. "The only time you ever saw him outside of the ball park was on the train or in the dining room. He never mixed with the players, but at the same time he always had tremendous morale on his clubs. He knew how to handle men. He was very shrewd, and gentle, and always talked to you like a father. The boys worshipped him."[9]

Although Mack was a gentleman, nothing pleased him more than being a successful thief. Because he had been a catcher, he was able to teach his base runners how to steal the enemy backstop's signals to his pitcher. More than one Philadelphia batter with a sure triple hauled up short at second to flash the batter a sign what pitch was coming next, thereby keeping an A's rally going. After trading a player, particularly a smart one, to an American League rival, Mack would often use his old set of signals to let the discarded man think he was stealing them. Then, with the game on the line, Mack would either change the signals or have one of his benchwarmers flash the real signs while he gave a decoy. Late in Mack's career, he pulled this stunt on Jimmy Dykes, after the old Athletics' third baseman became the playing-manager of the White Sox. After stealing signs the whole game, Dykes caught a signal for a bunt late in the game and charged the plate, only to have a ground smash go through him for the winning run.[10]

By 1910, so established was Mack's reputation as a sign stealer that the Cubs blamed their loss to the A's in the five-game World Series on Mack's thievery. Cub pitchers insisted that all their signs were being telegraphed by their catching staff. In fact, after the series, angry Chicago manager Frank Chance peddled his catcher, John Kling, to Boston. But Christy Mathewson, the great New York pitcher, credited Mack's superior strategy as the real reason for the Philadelphia win. "The Chicago pitchers were way off form in the series and could not control the ball, thus getting themselves 'in the hole' all the time," said Matty. "Shrewd Connie Mack soon realized this and ordered his batters to wait everything out, to make the twirlers throw every ball possible. The result was that, with the pitcher continually in the hole, the batters were guessing what was coming and frequently guessing right, as any smart hitter could under the circumstances. This made it look as if the Athletics were getting the Cubs' signals."[11]

Mack's 1911 club also won the American League flag—this time by thirteen and a half games over Ty Cobb and his Detroit Tigers' teammates. "[On] that team Connie Mack had practically everything that is needed for a great club," said New York manager John McGraw. "There were no weak spots that one could indicate with certainty . . . I have no hesitation in expressing the opinion that the Athletics of that period were one of the greatest ball clubs of all times."[12] Mack said his infield, made up of first baseman Stuffy McInnis, second baseman Eddie Collins, shortstop Jack Barry, and "Home Run" Baker, was worth $100,000—a huge sum in those preinflationary times. The A's disposed of John McGraw's Giants in a six-game World Series, limiting New York to an anemic .175 batting average.

Moreover, Mack successfully ordered his team to set up a defense against base stealing, the Giants' main strength. "Mack's pitchers cut their motions down to nothing with men on the bases . . . and they watched the runners like hawks," said New York's Christy Mathewson ruefully. "McGraw, with his all-star cast of thieves, was stopped in the World Series by one Cornelius McGillicuddy."[13]

The 1912 season was a disappointment for Mack, whose A's fell to third place despite a club he then claimed was his best ever. He blamed the loss on overconfidence and the loss of a lucky pencil he used to mark his scorecard. The year 1913 again belonged to the Athletics, and once again the Mackmen trounced the mighty Giants as the aging Plank bested Mathewson 3–1 in the fifth-game finale. But the 1914 season spelled nothing but unpleasantness for Mack. The mighty A's won the American League pennant, but the "Miracle Braves"—so called because Boston had been in last place on July 18—handily beat the Mackmen in a four-game upset. Worse, Mack heard awful, though unproven, rumors that members of his A's had thrown the series at the behest of gamblers. Then the manager lost hurler Chief Bender and Eddie Plank to the newly formed (and short-lived) Federal League, and the manager sold the contracts of Eddie Collins (to the White Sox), Jack Barry (to the Red Sox) and Home Run Baker (to the Yankees) in a move to keep the veterans in the American League. It was 1929 before Mack could build another world champion team.

Although it had been fifteen years since he'd managed in a World Series, Mack had lost none of his spirit, astounding his opponents, the mighty Cubs, with his strategy. Usually the A's manager played conservative baseball, refusing, for example, to ever yank a pitcher who was behind by one run in a low-scoring game until the eighth or ninth inning. But if a rival club became complacent, he delighted in trying something sensational. As a case in point, Mack had won the 1929 American League pennant behind the pitching of George Earnshaw (24–8), Lefty Grove (20–6), and Rube Walberg (18–11), but he chose not to start any of his three big guns in the opening game against Chicago. Instead, he surprised the Cubs by opening with an over-the-hill veteran named Howard Ehmke, who had skipped the last week of the season to scout the Cubs for Mack.

The psychological ploy worked. Chicago was flabbergasted to see that their opponent was a thirty-five-year-old has-been who had pitched in only eleven games that season. But Mack had wisely kept the old timer rested, and squeezed seven important victories out of him during the regular season. Ehmke's success helped him become a World Series legend and supported Mack's contention that "pitching is 75 percent of baseball." Ehmke's tantalizing slow curves and offspeed pitches helped him fan thirteen Cubs—then a series record—en route to a 3–1 win over Chicago's ace Charlie Root.

According to Cub manager Joe McCarthy, Mack hadn't even told his A's who would start in the opener. "When they saw Ehmke go out to warm up, some of the A's said, 'My God, are we going to work *him*?' " recalled McCarthy. "[But] Connie never blinked an eye; he knew what he was doing. You see, Ehmke had a delivery that was rough on right-handed hitters, and we were loaded with them."[14]

But what most have forgotten is that Mack pulled one pitching surprise after another against the Cubs. Mack's second surprise came when he decided not to start Walberg and Grove but to use his aces strictly in relief the entire 1929 series. Mack pitched the fireballing Grove in the fifth inning of game two in relief of Earnshaw to save an easy 9–3 win. "There wasn't a thing we could do with him," lamented McCarthy.[15] By yanking Earnshaw early, Mack was able to try another ploy by pitching his ace again with only two days rest in game three. The bold move almost worked. Earnshaw pitched a valiant game for nine innings, but unfortunately for the A's, Chicago bunched three runs together off him in the sixth for a 3–1 Cub victory.

That same 1929 series demonstrated the wisdom of Mack, who always insisted that no enemy lead was too big to overcome. In game four, the A's were down 8–0 in the seventh. But thanks to a Philadelphia barrage of hits and two balls lost in the sun by Cub outfielder Hack Wilson, the A's scored ten runs in the bottom of the seventh to trounce the disheartened Chicagoers, 10–8.

The A's repeated as world champions against the St. Louis Cardinals in 1930 and added an American League pennant in 1931. The American League teams were led by such heavy hitters as Jimmie Foxx, Al Simmons, and Mickey Cochrane, all destined for Cooperstown.

But the glory years were over for Mack, although he was honored by induction into the Hall of Fame in 1937 while still active as a manager. During his long career,

Connie Mack had his share of failure as well as triumph. The 4,025 games his teams lost is a major-league record. Moreover, in seventeen out of his fifty-three seasons as a manager, he piloted last place clubs. Writer Wilfred Sheed once wisecracked that Mack's lean years "tended to linger a bit like biblical plagues." More often than not, the Athletics were under-bankrolled, and Mack had to make do with marginal players. But his contribution to the game went far beyond mere wins and losses. He helped convert a game for toughs and gamblers into a sport for families to enjoy. When he retired at the end of the 1950 season, the world of baseball said a tearful goodbye. On February 8, 1956, the world wept once again when Cornelius McGillicuddy—the man known everywhere as "Mr. Baseball"—died at ninety-three of complications from a fractured hip.

$\diamondsuit$ 3 $\diamondsuit$ FRANK CHANCE: THE PEERLESS LEADER

During the first decade of the twentieth century, Chicago Cubs manager Frank Leroy Chance was more popular than the leading men of the silent screen era. Blessed with the body and good looks of a sculptor's model, the 6′1″, 196-pound Chance was one of the most impressive-looking men ever to play and manage the game.

In an April 19, 1913, *Collier's* magazine article, writer Will Irwin provided an engaging description of Chance's Herculean build. "A man in summer clothes, hung over a frame which would make you turn in a crowd, was leaning against one of the piazza pillars [in Bermuda's New Brunswick Hotel lobby]," wrote Irwin. "A pair of wide shoulders topped an ample chest which ran down to a torso as flat and supple as a boy's. . . . He looked as though a mountain might fall on him and crack his torso without ever jarring those sturdy props. He had a fine and full head, set on a powerful back neck, an aquiline nose that began massive and ran down to a fine point, a wide, firm mouth . . . and clear, hazel-grey eyes, set in little sun wrinkles."

The story of Frank Chance began with his birth in Fresno, California, on September 9, 1877, where he was educated in that city's public schools. Unlike many ball-players who view the game as a means of escaping poverty, the young man came from a wealthy background. His father was president of the First National Bank of Fresno until he died prematurely in 1891.

Two years after burying his father, Chance enrolled at Washington College in Irvington, California. Younger than many fellow students but already blessed with the build of a man, he played catcher for the Irvington varsity for three seasons (1893–95), while studying dentistry. Chance quit the university without graduating before the start of his senior year to accept an offer to play semi-professional baseball, immediately thrusting him into the role of his family's black sheep. The $40-per-month offer for the 1896 season came from a former Irvington team-mate, Rod Wagner, manager of the Sullivan, Illinois, club. Family pressure forced him to enroll in college once more in 1897, but he played baseball on weekends for the am-ateur Fresno team. A right-handed thrower who batted from the right side, he came to the attention of profes-sional scouts when he batted .479 in a fifty-team Pacific Coast Amateur Championship Tournament, leading his team to a third-place finish.[1]

Chance received offers from New York, Baltimore, and Chicago—the latter on the recommendation of former Cub outfielder Bill Lange who saw the boy play for Fresno. Baltimore outbid Chicago by more than $300 per month, but Chance signed for $1,200 a year with Cap Anson's Windy City team because he felt he had a better chance to make the first nine.

Anson was fired shortly before Chance joined the team and was replaced by Tommy Burns. When the 6′, 190-pounder joined the club in the spring of 1898, he was promptly dubbed "Husk" (short for "Husky") in honor of his size. Although Chance demonstrated that he had speed on the base paths, he proved incompetent as a catcher, winding up with broken fingers on passed balls and used only to "mop up" games already won or lost. Discouraged by his inability to replace first-string catcher Tim Donahue, he told his manager that he planned to quit the team, but a pep talk by sportswriter Speed Johnson changed Chance's mind.[2]

Fortunately for the youngster, Burns departed in 1902, and his replacement, Frank Selee, installed Chance at first base. Under Selee, Chance became part of an infield combination that was celebrated in verse by New York *Evening Mail* writer Franklin P. Adams, following a dazzling double play by Chicago that led to a Giants' defeat.

> *These are the saddest of possible words—*
> *Tinker to Evers to Chance.*
> *Trio of Bear Cubs and fleeter than birds—*
> *Tinker to Evers to Chance.*
> *Thoughtlessly pricking our gonfalon bubble,*
> *Making a Giant hit into a double.*
> *Words that are weighty with nothing but trouble—*
> *Tinker to Evers to Chance.*

Although Chance balked at playing first base until ordered to do so by Selee, he thrived by playing daily. His career average was under .300 his first four seasons, but at age twenty-five, he batted .327 in 1903, stealing a league-leading sixty-seven bases. Ironically, despite his size, the cleanup-hitting Chance failed to hit for power. He always choked up several inches on the bat and poked just two home runs that year—second to catcher Johnny Kling with three—on a Cub roster that collectively hit only nine homers. In 1904, Chance became team captain, hitting .310.

In 1905, the tuberculosis-ridden Selee departed the team halfway through the season, and in a player vote, Frank Chance became the new Cub manager. The team, inspired by the hard-driving "Peerless Leader" as sportswriter Charlie Dryden of the *Tribune* had dubbed him, won forty out of the final sixty-five games to finish third, while Chance batted .316 with ninety-two runs scored in only 392 at-bats.

In 1906, Chance could have been elected mayor of Chicago as the Cubs ended a streak of nineteen years without a pennant. Crowds estimated at 50,000 began to gather around downtown bulletin boards, where highlights of the game were posted. The club's 116 wins (against a mere 36 losses) eclipsed the old major-league record of 106 set two years earlier by John McGraw's Giants. Moreover, in this age of parity baseball, it's a record that likely never will be broken. McGraw's 1906 Giants finished in second place with ninety-six wins, twenty games back of the Cubs.

Why was the team so good? According to the *Reach Official Guide* [to baseball] (1907), "The Chicago team far outclassed any of its competitors in every department of play." The *Guide* lauded "the best pitching corps of any club, two of the best catchers in the profession" (wisely platooned by Chance), a fast fielding and hard hitting infield and outfield, more than the average number of quick thinkers and fast base runners." Ironically, it was the member of the infield who was uncelebrated in light verse—third baseman Harry Steinfeldt—who led the Cubbies in hitting with a .327 average. Chance himself hit .319, and again led the league in stolen bases with fifty-seven.

Moreover, Chance's leadership helped create one of the most harmonious teams in the history of the game. Petty differences evaporated as the team pulled together to annihilate the opposition. Continued the *Guide*: "the team played clean as well as aggressive ball, and was entirely free from public or private rows or scandals, and was in every way a credit to Chicago, the National League, and the profession."

Chance's own prowess on the base paths rubbed off on his players. His steal sign seemed forever on as Chicago stole 283 bases in 1906, with seven men stealing at least twenty-five bases. He urged his team to play heads-up ball, and once, against Cincinnati, he alertly scored from second base on a sacrifice bunt when the pitcher lobbed the ball to first for the putout. So impressed were owners Charles Taft and Charles Webb Murphy that they offered on the spot to sell him 10 percent of the Cubs for $10,000—well below the club's market value.

Although the Cubs were short on power, team members had a knack for getting on base, leading the National League in batting with a .262 average, as well as in hits, RBIs, triples, slugging and fielding percentage (a .969 mark, which was then a major-league record), and runs scored. Chance's pitching corps included three twenty-game winners ("Three Finger" Brown, Jack Pfiester, and Ed Reulbach), two seventeen-game winners, and two twelve-game winners. Unfortunately, the overconfident Cubs went down to a World Series defeat at the hands of their crosstown rivals, the anemic-hitting White Sox, who suddenly became terrors at the plate to win in six games.

Nonetheless, this Cubby team went on to enjoy the modern era's first baseball dynasty, winning four pennants in five seasons. The club again performed brilliantly under its fiery playing-manager, winning the pennant by seventeen games ahead of second-place Pittsburgh. Chance was ahead of his time, always trying to win psychological edges—such as taking advantage of a rule [changed in 1950] that allowed the home team to bat first if it so chose—if he thought his club could touch an inexperienced pitcher for a couple of quick runs. Moreover, Chance—the converted first baseman—led the league in fielding percentage. And in October, the Cubs turned into full-grown grizzlies, demolishing the Detroit Tigers in five games.

By 1908 the Cubs were the equivalent of the latter-day Yankees. Chance's Chicagoans believed that winning by one run was as good as winning by ten. The manager "relied on the sacrifice and steal," said utility player Jimmy Archer. "He played for that one run that would win the game."[3]

National-League teams threw their best pitchers at the Cubs, but still Chicago prevailed. Unfortunately, the good will on the team of earlier years had been replaced by dissension. When the team dropped out of first place temporarily, the New York *Evening Mail* couldn't resist taking this potshot at Chance on July 24, 1908: "At a banquet in New York last December, Johnny Evers declared that the absolute lack of friction between members of the Chicago team was responsible for its lack of success, and that Frank Chance was like a father to the boys . . . Perhaps Chance has [now] become a stepfather. After a game lost this season Chance yelled at his men, 'You're a fine lot of curs, you are.' Not exactly the sort of talk boys expect from their father. Rumor has it that 'curs' was not the word used, but it will do under the circumstances."

What had happened was that Chance, now thirty, had become somewhat withdrawn and ill-tempered, perhaps because he saw himself as a team elder statesman but more likely as a result of some serious beanings he took. Like Don Baylor of Oakland today, Chance never lost an opportunity to take a free base if he could manage to put his body in the path of the ball, but unfortunately, he had beanballs in the head that he should have ducked. Some evidence of his now-unyielding nature occurred in mid-season when he forbade a player named Artie "Circus Solly" Hofman from marrying his fiancé, Rae Looker, until after the season was over. Hofman protested vehemently, but Chance, as usual, could not be moved. The strictest disciplinarian in the game, the manager was famous for his 11:30 P.M. curfews.

Although he stole only twenty-seven bases and his average plummetted to .272, Chance continued to inspire his teammates on the field. The manager's philosophy was that he who managed best managed least. He was a stickler for physical conditioning and ordered his players to drink moderately but otherwise gave few orders. The Cubs ate and drank together, and the topic Chance always brought up was baseball: how to pitch to so-and-so, how to get the best jump on a pitcher, what to do in a given situation. He had confidence in his players and relied on their judgment. "I was picking up a bat one day," recalled Jimmy Archer of the Cubs, "[and] I said to Chance, 'What do you want me to do?' He said, 'You're over 21. Go up there and see what you can do.' "[4]

According to Edwin Pope, author of *Baseball's Greatest Managers* (1960), Chance originated the strategy to thwart a sacrifice bunt with men on first and second. "Shortstop Joe Tinker would pester the runner at second," wrote Pope. "When the ball was hit, the pitcher would bounce off the mound toward third and Chance would sprint in from first. The third baseman played close enough to the bag to take a throw for the force. The strength of the maneuver lay in holding the runner so close to second that he couldn't get a jump to third base."

Chance always gave his players a chance to fail, believing that they were the best judge of their own moods and talents. "He didn't tell you what to do," Jimmy Archer explained. "If you made a mistake, he pointed it out later."[5]

The 1908 season went down to a dogfight for the pennant among Chicago, New York, and Pittsburgh. Chance won several important games with his alertness and his glove. The first took place at the Polo Grounds against hated New York on September 23, with only percentage points separating the Giants and Cubs. With two outs in the ninth, men on first and third, Al Bridwell of the Giants singled to center to apparently win the game, 2–1. But

Chance alertly noticed that the New York runner, Fred Merkle, had stopped short of second when the run scored and had made a beeline for the clubhouse. The manager screamed at his center fielder, Artie Hofman, to throw the ball to second, but the errant throw went by Johnny Evers, and a New York coach, Iron Man McGinnity, intercepted it. And when Chance and two Cubs tried to wrench the ball from the coach's grasp, the ball squirted into a crowd of New York fans, who had joyfully overrun the field.

What happened next was chronicled by Charles Dryden of the *Tribune*: "It [the ball] rolled among the spectators who had swarmed upon the diamond like an army of starving potato bugs. At this thrilling juncture, Kid Kroh, the demon [Chicago] southpaw, swarmed upon the human potato bugs and knocked six of them galley-west. . . . The ball was conveyed to Evers for the forceout of Merkle. . . . Some say Merkle eventually touched second base, but not until he had been forced out by Hofman to McGinnity, to six potato bugs, to Kroh, to some more Cubs, and the shrieking, triumphant Mr. Evers." Confusion reigned on the field, and the next day the umpires declared a tie, with National League president Henry Clay Pulliam saying that the game had to be replayed on October 8.

But before that day, the Pirates still needed to be dealt with. On October 4, according to writer Hugh S. Fullerton of the New York *American*, in the eighth inning, Chance made "one of the most astounding plays ever" to choke a Pittsburgh rally in the eighth. According to Fullerton, "[Tommy] Leach hit a fierce line drive straight over first, and it looked a sure double until Chance, with a running jump, shoved out one hand, turned backwards and clung to the ball," ensuring a 5–2 win. "An hour after the game was done a thousand fans still waited outside the park. As Chance backed his automobile out, hundreds swarmed around him, cheering wildly."

The 1908 season ended climactically on October 8 as Three Finger Brown relieved Jack Pfeister and ended the Giants' hopes and Christy Mathewson's bid for a thirty-eighth win by shutting down McGraw's men, 4–2. Before the game, Chance tangled with Iron Man McGinnity over the "potato bug" affair, but the manager kept his composure, belting three hits in the game. Then, as Chance was walking off the field, a cowardly fan punched him in the throat, smashing the cartilage in his neck. Shaking off the effects of the blow, Chance played two days later in the World Series opener against Detroit. In the series, won four games to one by the Cubs, Chance led both teams with a .421 batting average.

The following year Chicago won 104 games, but partially because of the loss of star catcher Johnny Kling in a contract dispute, Chance's Cubs finished second to Pittsburgh by six and a half games. Kling returned in 1910, and the Cubs easily won the National League flag by thirteen games. But Connie Mack's Philadelphia Athletics, behind the .400 batting of Eddie Collins and Frank Baker, beat the Cubs in the World Series in five games. Plagued by headaches and double vision as the result of being hit thirty-seven times in the head while at bat, Chance saw only part-time duty in 1910 and called it quits the following season.

Perhaps because his fading health made him more and more irritable, Chance began feuding with owners Charles Murphy and Charles Taft. The manager once grew so angry after a winning streak ended that he crushed a piano in the clubhouse with a baseball bat. He sometimes fought two of his players in one day, and even the crusty veteran Honus Wagner labeled him one of the three toughest managers of all time.

Nonetheless, he could be surprisingly gentle in handling a rookie. On Opening Day in 1912, Chance sent newcomer Jimmy Lavender to the mound to pitch in relief against future Hall-of-Famer Honus Wagner. "You can imagine how I felt," Lavender told sportswriter Edwin Pope years later. "I'd never pitched in a big-league game, and here Chance was putting me in against the greatest National League hitter of that time and perhaps all time. But Chance kept talking, cooling me down, building me up. Finally he said, 'Jimmy, just waste a few on Wagner, then pitch him down the middle, waist-high, with not too much on it.' " Lavender pitched as ordered, retired Wagner on a fly, and went on to win sixteen games as a rookie.

But such successes were not enough to preserve Chance's job. When the Cubs finished second in 1911 and third in 1912, President Murphy ousted the man who had brought four pennants to Chicago, and whose winning percentage was a sparkling .665 (753–379). Thanks to that tenth interest he had purchased in 1906, Chance departed the team with a check for $140,000—big money in that era—looking like the picture of a successful businessman, smoking an expensive pipe and driving an ultraluxurious Blitzen-Benz automobile.

In spite of declining health the rest of his life, Chance attempted several managerial comebacks, with the New York Yankees (1913–1914) and the Boston Red Sox (1923), but finished in the second division with both clubs. "A manager can only do so much," said Lefty O'Doul, a member of the Red Sox under Chance. "Take Frank Chance. One of the greatest, right? . . . Well, in 1923 we ended dead last. Just proves if you haven't got the horses you haven't got a Chance. [O'Doul's pun intended]"[6]

In 1924, the White Sox offered Chance an opportunity to return to the Windy City as manager, but by then his ill health had reached the point of no return. A brain operation was required, the result of so many pitched balls he took in the head, and his hearing failed him. He died at the age of forty-seven on September 14, 1924, but was recognized for his accomplishments as baseball's finest player-manager when he was posthumously elected to the Hall of Fame in 1946.

4 ◇ JOHN JOSEPH McGRAW: THE LITTLE NAPOLEON

John McGraw not only possessed what players in his day called "baseball savvy," he also had enough grit to enforce his edicts. This twentieth-century tyrant stood but 5′7″ tall and weighed only 120 pounds at the start of his baseball career. There was never anyone like this angry New Yorker who kept a wildcat for a pet and dressed more suavely than the city's mayors. Even after he gained considerable girth around his midsection, sportswriters covering his New York Giants referred to the self-assured McGraw as the "Little Napoleon."

McGraw ran a far from benevolent dictatorship from the dugout. He insisted upon signaling to his players both at bat and in the field on practically every pitch, using such signs as touching his shoelaces or blowing his nose. "Our success can be laid to the fact . . . that I had absolute confidence in our players and they had a similar confidence in me," explained McGraw.[1]

The manager wouldn't tolerate anyone who failed to live by the rules. A player who disregarded a signal could expect a tongue lashing, a demotion, or an instant trade.

In 1905, a Giant hitter named Sammy Strang ignored McGraw's bunt sign and clubbed a home run to right, knocking in two men on base for the winning runs. After tipping his cap to the roaring New York crowd, Strang ran into his scowling manager's fury.

"That'll cost you twenty-five," growled McGraw. "Didn't you have instructions to bunt that ball?"

"Sure, but say, Mac—that one came over there like a balloon," whimpered Strang. "I just couldn't help taking a poke at it."

The angry manager slapped a $25 fine on Strang, the equivalent of a whopping fine in those days of minuscule salaries. "All right," said Strang in a resigned voice. "But the way that one felt I guess it was worth it."[2]

Unlike many managers, McGraw refused to have one set of rules for stars, another set for bench warmers. He treated all his players the same, rarely playing favorites even among players he adored, such as Christy Mathewson and Mel Ott. One of his greatest players—future Hall of Fame second basemen Frankie Frisch—was booted off the team by the red-faced manager. Frisch, the Giants' captain in 1926, became the frequent target of McGraw's blistering tongue and jumped the team during a late-season road trip. The manager promptly traded him to St. Louis where his hustling tactics helped him fit in well as a member of the Cardinals' so-called Gashouse Gang. Ironically, Hornsby came to New York from St. Louis in that trade and lasted only one year under McGraw before being peddled to the Boston Braves. Hornsby was dismissed for trying to persuade Giant owner Charles Stoneham to fire McGraw and hire him.

McGraw was always an obstinate character, even as a boy. A second-generation Irishman, John Joseph McGraw was born in Truxton, New York—a tiny town located on the east branch of the Tioughnioga River—on April 7, 1873, to John and Ellen McGraw. The family was split up after the deaths of Ellen and four of the children due to a diphtheria epidemic, and twelve-year-old John was taken in by relatives. The boy's relationship with his father was always stormy. The elder John—a railroad laborer—regarded his boy's love of baseball as a disgraceful waste of time and beat him once for disregarding an order not to play and shattering windows on a church located in right center with some sandlot blasts. The boy's solution at age sixteen was not to give up his beloved sport but to learn how to place his hits to left, a practice that later helped him perfect the hit-and-run play.

Because his immigrant father didn't think much of schoolwork, John quit his studies while only in his teens and went to work selling candy on the Elmira, Cortland, and Northern Railroad line. But in defiance of his father, he pitched for the Truxton Grays and other town teams. The boy's break came when Albert Kenney, a Truxton resident who worked as manager of Olean in the New York and Pennsylvania leagues, signed him to a $40 a month contract in 1890. Kenney converted McGraw from a pitcher to a third baseman, but he lost faith in the player and John wound up with Wellsville in the Western New York League, hitting .365 and winning a promotion to Cedar Rapids in the Illinois-Iowa League. His splendid play caught the attention of the Baltimore Orioles manager Billy Barnie, and in August 1891, he joined the major leagues to stay for more than four decades as a player and manager.

As a third baseman on a great Baltimore team, with such noted teammates as catcher Wilbert Robinson, shortstop Hughey Jennings, and outfielder Willie Keeler, the fiery McGraw became famous for playing with pain. He once played for weeks with a splintered collar bone. Like Ty Cobb, McGraw was said to sharpen his spikes before a game to teach infielders to respect his slides into bases. "The main idea is to win," McGraw liked to say, parlaying that simple philosophy into a terrific career as a player and later as a manager. Behind his back, both opponents and teammates referred to the pugnacious McGraw as Muggsy, after a roughneck Baltimore politician who shared the manager's last name.[3] McGraw hated the name.

In his career as a player (primarily as a third baseman), which lasted from 1891 to 1906, McGraw collected a career batting average of .334, helping the Baltimore Orioles to pennants in 1894, 1895, and 1896. On the field he showed himself a master of baseball strategy, inventing several plays that eventually became part of the game's fundamentals. He used his ability to place hits, gained while avoiding church windows as a youngster, to perfect the art of the hit-and-run, a skill he used often at Baltimore while batting behind Willie Keeler, the sawed-off player whose simple secret to batting success was "to hit 'em where they ain't." He and Keeler also excelled at both bunting and hitting behind the runner to advance him. Both men also perfected the art of fouling off a dozen or more pitches in a single at bat, managing to either draw a walk or tire out a pitcher so that someone else down the batting order could get to him.

One strategy that McGraw employed as a third baseman was far from sportsmanlike in that era when only one umpire worked a game. Whenever a man was on third and a batter lofted a potential sacrifice fly, McGraw would sneak behind the runner to snag hold of his belt while the umpire's eyes were on the catch. That loss of a precious second trapped more than one outraged runner at the plate, causing the major leagues to adopt a second umpire to keep an eye on such shenanigans.

In 1899, the feisty McGraw became playing-manager of Baltimore, then in the soon-to-fold American Association. He bounced like a yo-yo the next few years, playing ninety-nine games in the National League in 1900 for the St. Louis Cardinals, moving back to Baltimore in 1901 to manage the upstart American League's entry there, and, in 1902 (the same year he married the former Blanche

Sindall), midway through the season, abandoning Baltimore for the New York Giants of the National League. This last move was permanent. He remained in the Big Apple with the Giants—precursor of the club now based in San Francisco—until poor health forced him out thirty years later.

In 1903, his first full season with the Giants, McGraw gave indications of future greatness by piloting what had been a perennial second-division team to a second-place finish. The star of the club was Christy Mathewson, destined to win 373 games and who was as much a gentleman as McGraw was a street fighter. But the two men and their wives got along famously, even to the point of sharing an apartment together. Both possessed a mutual love of winning, whether it be baseball or checkers—the latter a game in which Mathewson excelled, beating many midwestern champions. One day, reported the pitcher, McGraw declared he'd cut off the fingers of all his pitchers if he thought it would make them hurl as effectively as the aptly named Mordecai "Three-Finger" Brown, the Chicago Cubs star in four pennant-winning years.

From McGraw, the 6'1½" Mathewson learned about the inside game of baseball. He learned how to outwait spitball pitchers such as Russell Ford of the New York Highlanders, knowing that the strain of throwing such a pitch made Ford vulnerable to Giant bats in the late innings. McGraw also stressed the importance of base stealing and could never really adjust to the "big inning" concept of baseball that Babe Ruth introduced in the early 1920s. His best team for thefts was the 1911 club, which stole 347 bases, a major-league record. His ideal game was one in which he scored the most runs on the fewest hits. The manager believed that raw speed had very little to do with smart baserunning.

"Get the start," McGraw told Mathewson and his teammates. "Half of base stealing is leaving the bag at the right time. Know when you have a good lead and then never stop until you have hit the dirt."[4]

In 1904 and 1905, behind Mathewson and the unyielding arm of pitcher Joe "Iron Man" McGinnity, McGraw won the hearts of all New Yorkers by pushing, shoving, and exhorting his Giants to two pennant-winning seasons. In 1905, the Giants never relinquished control of first place after April 23.

McGraw's knowledge of all facets of the game made him immensely respected during the first two decades of his career. He could teach a veteran pitcher such as Burleigh Grimes "a whole new theory of curve ball pitching in about five minutes." He showed Grimes how to make right-handed batters ground into double plays and taught him "little things that changed careers around."[5]

McGraw maintained that he owed his success to his insistence upon employing smart players on the ballfield who paid attention to the little things. Given a choice, he always signed a college-educated player over one who starred on a town or factory team. He himself attended college for several years in the off-season at Allegany College (today called St. Bonaventure) outside Olean, New York. "The difference is simply this," argued McGraw. "The college boy, or anyone with even a partially trained mind, immediately tries to find his faults; the unschooled fellow usually tries to hide his. The moment a man locates his faults he can quickly correct them. The man who thinks he is keeping his mistakes under cover will never advance a single step until he sees the light."

McGraw added that players such as Honus Wagner and Tris Speaker, who never attended college, "had brains enough to see the handicap and through persistence and determination overcame it."[6]

McGraw's system relied upon ballplayers who could think. He came into the game while baseball was still young and imprinted his influence upon future strategies.

He was the first manager to abandon the coaching lines for the dugout, recognizing that he needed his full concentration on the game at all times. Coaching outside first or third base, McGraw believed, fragmented his attention.

The manager believed that conservative baseball was bad baseball. He played for the winning runs and took whatever gamble he needed to win. Once, before he took to the dugout to manage, he coached the Giants from third base while the team was losing by five runs in the ninth against the Cardinals. With a man on first and Red Murray on second, the Giants singled but McGraw forbade Murray from scoring. The manager felt that the sight of three dancing runners might rattle the St. Louis pitcher. The ploy succeeded, and McGraw strutted into the clubhouse, a winner once again.

McGraw's record during the second decade of this century was not enviable; his club won four pennants (1911, 1912, 1913, 1917) but lost all the series matchups. However, he regained his magic from 1921 to 1924, becoming the first modern manager to win four consecutive pennants and this time winning the world championship in 1921 and 1922. In 1923, he lost the World Series to the Yankees, and in 1924, to the Washington Senators, on a ground ball that rookie third baseman Freddy Lindstrom failed to nab as it took a bad hop over his head.

Although that 1924 pennant was the last he ever won, McGraw's word was absolute on the field throughout his career. Not even his players could guess his strategy. On rare occasions, he would break with traditional strategy, even allowing hitters to swing on a 3–0 pitch if he expected a balloon ball to float over the plate. During a 1921 series against Pittsburgh, for example, George "Highpockets" Kelly nearly swallowed his tongue when McGraw's coach, Hughie Jennings, flashed the hit sign on a three ball, no strike count, with the bases loaded and New York down 3–0. Pirate hurler Babe Adams grooved a pitch down the middle and Kelly took him downtown for a grand slam home run.

That hit took the heart out of the Pirates and McGraw knew it. After the game, the manager let everyone in earshot know about his strategy. "McGraw comes strutting in," said Kelly. " 'If my brains hold out,'—McGraw took one look at me—'we'll win it.' "[7] The Giants trounced Pittsburgh in five straight games.

The manager personally played a key strategic role again during the 1922 World Series. That season, McGraw invented the cutoff play from the outfield. Before this, outfielders traditionally tried to heave the ball more than three hundred feet on the fly to catch a runner at the plate, often allowing the hitter to advance a base. McGraw insisted that his outfielders throw to the shortstop, giving that man the option of whipping the ball home or firing to first in hopes of catching a runner who had rounded too far from the bag.

Although McGraw conceived the play during the 1922 regular season, the wily boss kept it under wraps until the World Series against the crosstown Yankees. His talented shortstop, Dave Bancroft, nailed three players who were trying to take an extra base on a throw from the outfield. By cutting the throw off, Bancroft conceded a run that likely would have scored anyway, but he prevented another runner from being in position to score on a single. That play broke the heart of three Yankee rallies and contributed to the Giants' defeat of New York in five games during the first World Series ever to be broadcast live on radio. All New York could manage was a tie in the second game of the series—a controversial game called by an umpire because of darkness even though the sun still hung in the sky.

Another contributing factor in that 1922 series was the handcuffing of mighty Babe Ruth by Giant pitchers. "All you need is to fool just one player—or maybe two,"

McGraw told his men. "One such move will often throw a monkey wrench into the whole machinery of the opposition." During the series, McGraw said, Ruth guessed correctly on no more than three balls. "If he looked for a slow one, invariably he would get something else. When he expected a fast one he would get a curve or a slow one. We had him completely at sea."[8]

Ruth looked like a bush-league rookie against the National Leaguers that series, chasing several pitches that were well outside the strike zone while McGraw and his men berated him from the bench for his ineptitude. "Lay it over for him," McGraw yelled at his pitcher, Art Nehf. "He can't hit it even if you tell him what's coming."[9] In seventeen at bats, Ruth failed to hit a home run, managing only a double and single for a .118 average with but one RBI.

McGraw's eye for baseball talent was legendary. One day during the 1925 season, a thick-legged Louisiana boy of sixteen stepped into McGraw's office, straw suitcase in hand. The stocky catcher had been sent by Harry Williams, only one of McGraw's many friends who kept an eye out for potential Giant talent. "Mister McGraw, I'm Mel Ott," the boy said, hoping his voice sounded less awed and frightened than he thought it did.

McGraw watched the boy take batting practice, scowling at the odd way the 5'9", 170-pounder lifted his front leg before lashing into the ball, but nodding with delight as pitch after pitch rocketed over the short Polo Grounds right field fence, only 257 feet from home plate. Pursing his lips, McGraw made two snap decisions. The first was to convert the boy to an outfielder, knowing that his small size and piano legs wouldn't take the punishment of year-in and year-out duty behind the plate. The second was to keep the boy on the bench with him during September of the 1925 season and use him sparingly the following season. He was biding his time until the kid was ready instead of sending him down for seasoning.

"That's the best natural swing I've seen in years," McGraw told an underling. "And I'm not going to let some fool minor-league manager ruin that kid by changing his style. I'm going to keep him myself."[10]

McGraw acted as a surrogate father to the boy, even fining him $100 for playing poker with the veterans because the manager thought him too young to gamble. He picked just the right games and situations for Ott to build the boy's confidence. During the 1926 season, the seventeen-year-old outfielder hit .383 in sixty times at bat. In 1927, he batted .282 in eighty-two games, legging out an inside-the-park homer. Before his career ended, Ott held the National League record for career home runs with 511, finishing his playing career in 1946. In 1951, McGraw's ability to see and effectively use talent was recalled by all baseball observers when the former boy wonder, Mel Ott, made the Hall of Fame.

Unfortunately, Ott starred for McGraw during the manager's years of decline. Even the Little Napoleon met his Waterloo. From 1925 to 1931, McGraw's last full season, the Giants finished second three times, third three times, and fifth once. Losing did not become the manager, and he became more profane and impatient with his players as the all-important National League pennant kept eluding him. On June 3, 1932, McGraw's possibly stress-induced prostate cancer forced him from the game, and his great first baseman, Bill Terry, succeeded him.

In 1933, McGraw had a fleeting return to glory when he managed the first National League All-Star team. That year, the Giants won not only the pennant but also the World Series, with Mel Ott booming a home run in the tenth inning of the final game to defeat the Washington Senators. McGraw watched his team play from a clubhouse window in deep centerfield, reduced to the status of spectator. A few months later, on February 22, 1934, the sixty-year-old McGraw passed away of cancer and uremia.

"The Old Man," as his players had derisively begun calling him, had no reason to apologize for his career. In twenty-eight full seasons with New York, he missed the first division only twice. John McGraw's legacy won him election posthumously to the Hall of Fame in 1937.

5 MILLER HUGGINS: THE MIGHTY MITE

Perhaps Miller James Huggins was fortunate that he was reared in Cincinnati's fourth ward, a bad neighborhood where trouble could always be bought cheaply. The 5'4", 125-pound Huggins was destined to face trouble most of his life, but thanks to his natural intelligence and determination, he usually triumphed. Huggins was the first in the noble lineage of great Yankee skippers, managing such New York notables as Babe Ruth, Waite Hoyt, and Lou Gehrig. But despite all the talent on the Yankees his job was never easy. Almost to a man the players resented the diminutive man they scornfully called "The Flea" when he first took the post, and he had to quell several mutinies before he finally convinced them that a small man could be a big leader. In his dozen years with New York he won six pennants, and had he not died while in the prime of his life, there is no doubt he would have won a half-dozen more.

Born on March 27, 1880, to devout Methodist grocers of British ancestry, Huggins dutifully obeyed his parents until they forbade him to play baseball on Sundays for religious reasons. Even then his defiance went only so far. He played under a pseudonym, "Proctor," and tried to please his father by studying law at the University of Cincinnati. However, the lure of baseball eventually caused him to fly in the face of his family's wishes, and he signed a professional contract in 1899, with Mansfield of the Inter-State League, continuing his legal studies in the off-season. Hoping to offset the stigma of his frail frame, he built up his biceps and forearms with weights, occasionally managing to surprise opposing teams by belting a home run.

Huggins hit impressively in the minors, batting .322 in 1901 (Western League), and .328 and .308 against American Association pitchers in 1902 and 1903. When Cincinnati signed him to a major-league pact after the 1903 season, manager Joe Kelley boasted, "I've got a second baseman who'll make you all forget Bid McPhee (former seventeen-year veteran with Cincinnati)—Miller Huggins."[1]

While Kelley's praise of Huggins turned out to be exaggerated, the second baseman performed well at bat, hitting .263 and even smacking two home runs. His fielding was so exemplary that teammates referred to him as "Little Mr. Everywhere." Huggins lasted fourteen years as a player with Cincinnati and the St. Louis Cardinals (1910 to 1916), hitting as high as .292 in 1906.

As a player Huggins' strategy was to get on base any way he could and advance on a sacrifice or by stealing second. He never hesitated to sacrifice his own at-bat to move a teammate to the next base. On June 1, 1901, he set a record with six unofficial times at bat (two sacrifices and four walks) in a single game.

Quiet and never profane, the well-bred Huggins contrasted with the heavy-drinking, foul-mouthed players who populated big-league rosters back then. More for his manners than for his baseball knowledge, St. Louis owner Helene Britton appointed him the player-manager of the

Cards in 1913. Saddled with an untalented squad, Huggins managed the team to third place in the standings in 1914, the highest in the team's thirty-eight-year history.

On occasion, Huggins demanded more of himself as a player than he could deliver. His aging legs no longer responded as they once had when he tried to steal, and he set an unenviable record for most times being thrown out with thirty-six failed attempts. When a talented youngster named Rogers Hornsby joined the Cards in 1916, destined to win six National League batting titles, Huggins sat himself down on the bench. The so-called "Mighty Mite's" career batting average was .265, and all but 205 of his 1,474 hits were singles.

Though the Cardinals finished third in five years under Huggins, the manager was respected by his peers for his intelligence. Like a chess player, Huggins always seemed to be several moves ahead. Once, in a game against Philadelphia, Huggins—coaching at third—demanded that a rookie pitcher throw him the baseball half a dozen times, claiming that the kid was doctoring it. Knowing he was innocent of the charge, the pitcher complied, and after Huggins and the umpire had inspected the ball to their satisfaction, the manager always threw it back to the Philadelphian.

Late in the game, with Cardinal runners on second and third, Huggins asked to see the ball. The rookie impatiently lobbed it over to the coach, whereby Huggins stepped aside to let the ball roll all the way to the grandstand while the winning runs dashed merrily around the base paths.

In 1918 Huggins was unemployed, replaced by former Browns manager Branch Rickey after Britton sold the team to James C. Jones. That year, the Yankees fired manager Wild Bill Donovan, and New York co-owners Colonel Jacob Ruppert and Tillinghast L'Hommedieu Huston disagreed over who his successor should be. Ruppert, president of the Yankees, wanted Huggins. He overruled Huston, the team's vice-president, who wanted to hire jolly Wilbert Robinson, manager of the Brooklyn Robins. Since Huston was off fighting World War I, Ruppert had his way and hired Huggins.

A bachelor whose only passion outside the game was the stock market, Huggins had a sharp wit that sophisticated New York sportswriters appreciated. Asked, for example, what a player needed when in a bad slump, Huggins replied, "a string of alibis."

When Huggins assumed the post, Yankee baseball was far from the established tradition it is today. John McGraw and his Giants held a stranglehold on the game's popularity in New York City, and many baseball experts predicted that the Yankees under McGraw would be at best a carbon copy of McGraw's club, winning one-run games by employing a strategy based on sacrifices, speed on the base paths, and heads-up baseball.

But Huggins was bright enough to see that the game had changed. Crowds flocked to the Polo Grounds (where both the Yankees and Giants played at the time) to see titanic home runs hit by the gargantuan likes of Boston's Babe Ruth. They wanted to cheer long drives that shattered empty seats when they landed, not watch balls dribble through the infield. Thus, after Huggins' Yankees had experienced disappointing fourth- and third-place finishes in 1918 and 1919 respectively, the manager boldly suggested that New York secure Ruth from the financially strapped Red Sox. The New York press had paid tribute to New York's batting lineup after the team led the American League in 1919 with forty-five team homers, and Huggins wisely deduced what the addition of Ruth's bat (twenty-nine homers in 1919) would mean in added wins. After receiving Boston's permission to speak with Ruth, Huggins personally signed the slugger to a two-year pact worth $41,000—twice what Ruth made in Boston but cheap at the price. The Yankees drew 282,000 fans in 1918 without him and 1,289,422 fans in 1920 with him.

Thanks to the introduction of the so-called livelier ball in 1920, made possible by the manufacturer's switch from American yarn to Australian yarn, Ruth gave Huggins an immediate return on his investment. Inspired by Ruth's fifty-four home runs, the Yankees finished with 115 team homers, sixty-five more than the next American League team's total home runs. The club finished third, three scant games behind front-running Cleveland, and a dynasty was about to begin the next year in New York, producing twenty-nine first-place finishes in forty-four years. Huggins became, in future Yankee manager Joe McCarthy's words, "the man who cut the Yankee pennant pattern."

In 1921, Ruth dominated the American League, belting fifty-nine home runs, accumulating 170 runs batted in, and hitting .378. Second in homers with twenty-four was Bob Meusel, the Yankees outfielder, and although no other Yankee was in double figures, the team clubbed 134 homers. The pitching staff was led by terrible-tempered Carl Mays, a submarine-style thrower with twenty-seven wins, and rebellious Waite Hoyt with nineteen. Huggins won his first pennant in New York, and fans began shifting allegiance from the Giants to the Yankees despite a win by McGraw's National Leaguers in an eight-game World Series.

But at no time could Huggins relax, secure in the knowledge that he had formed a dynasty. Players such as Mays insulted him and ridiculed his size, suggesting that he was something less than a man. Huston never lost an opportunity to remind Huggins that he was not the co-owner's choice for the job. Nonetheless, the Yankees won pennants from 1921 to 1923 and from 1926 to 1928, and while Huggins rightfully could have used the press to lambaste his enemies, he never resorted to underhanded tactics, although he did dump troublemakers like Mays at the first opportunity.

"He was a quiet man by nature," recalled one of his Yankees, Bob Shawkey. "He tended to keep things to himself—very seldom exploded about anything. I think in certain ways he patterned himself after Connie Mack. . . . Neither man would ever criticize you in front of the other players. If you made a mistake, Connie would call you in the office the next day and have a little talk. Hug was the same way."[2]

Gradually Huggins earned the respect of all baseball men for winning with a deck filled with jokers and knaves. "I know of no one who could have taken over a bunch of artificial prima donnas," said the New York *World Telegram*'s Joe Williams, "and turned them ultimately into a perfect, machinelike organism." Writer Arthur Mann agreed, calling Huggins the "unseen power" behind New York's success.

Only once did the manager admit that he would have preferred to win with a different team than the Bronx Bombers. "Do you know this team doesn't play my kind of baseball?" he said to a sportswriter. "By that, I mean the kind I played myself and liked to direct with the Cards. But a manager has his cards dealt to him, and he must play them. A team is like a bridge hand. You've got to get up your strongest suit. My strongest suit is a slugging attack."[3]

Despite the impressiveness of the Yankees' lineup, Huggins stressed the importance of practicing a play until it was second nature to a player. He taught shortstop Mark Koenig how to go to his left to snag would-be hits over the bag, and Koenig appreciated the assistance. "He made you feel like a giant," said the shortstop. "If you made a mistake, he took you aside the next day [or] called you into his office." The manager also worked with Gehrig on his deficiencies at first. "One thing Gehrig can't do right is come in on bunts," said Huggins in spring training one year. "He never knows when to come in and when to stay out and let the pitcher handle the bunts. We're working on that every day."[4]

Huggins had to uncharacteristically assert himself against Ruth in 1925, after the outfielder had ballooned to more than 270 pounds and had failed to hit a home run until June 11. Ruth had sunk so low that Huggins even pinch-hit Bobby Veach for him, hoping to appeal to the star's pride. Finally, with the team hopelessly out of first place, Huggins fined Ruth $5,000 and suspended him indefinitely when the outfielder showed up in St. Louis thirty minutes late for a game.

Only one player, Bob Shawkey, was in the clubhouse to witness Ruth's comeuppance. "Babe took his jacket out of the locker, put it on, and started to leave," recalled Shawkey. "Then he turned around and called Huggins every name under the sun. Hug got up and walked over to him—he was about half Babe's size—and said, 'Babe, some day you're going to thank me for what I'm doing now. You're never going to play another game for the New York Yankees until you straighten yourself out.'"[5]

Ruth tried everything to get the decision overruled. He appealed to Ruppert, general manager Ed Barrow, and even Commissioner Kenesaw Mountain Landis, but all stoutly backed Huggins. The outfielder apologized to the manager, but Huggins refused to accept it until he was certain Ruth's words were genuine. When the manager finally let Ruth play again, Ruth was a different person. He never again caused a serious problem.

Baseball critics generally agree that the 1927 Yankees in particular were Huggins' strongest team, and indeed, probably the best team ever assembled on a major-league diamond. The press dubbed the team's lineup "Murderer's Row," fielding such feared hitters as Ruth with sixty home runs, Bob Meusel, Lou Gehrig, Tony Lazzeri, Mark Koenig, Joe Dugan, and Earl Combs.

The 1927 Yankees strode into Pittsburgh the following season to play the National League champion Pirates, and Huggins devastated Pittsburgh with a psychological ploy.

During the first batting practice, the manager ordered his pitcher to groove pitch after pitch to the slugging Yankees. Ball after ball landed deep in the upper deck of right field (the only field to have stands) and beyond the distant fences in center and left field, stupefying the Pirates as they watched the show of strength. To further show his disdain, the manager opened with rookie George Pipgras on the mound instead of a frontline pitcher. Demoralized, Pittsburgh lost four straight to the Yankees while Huggins modestly gave credit for the wins to his team.

With such a magnificent lineup, Huggins' best strategy was to play for the big inning, although he never hesitated to send even Babe Ruth down to steal second when the club needed one run. Most baseball fans are surprised to learn that the powerfully built Ruth nonetheless stole 123 bases in his career. On occasion, if one run were needed to win the game, Huggins even ordered his slugger to bunt, and Ruth complied. "The team that wins is the one that makes the most of its abilities," maintained Huggins.

"Nothing ever missed his eye," Combs once said of him. "He was a genius at sensing what a rival manager was going to do. He just seemed to know when the other team was going to bunt or put on the hit-and-run."[6]

Huggins, ever the strategist, chose players who not only could hit a ball but catch and throw it, too. Ruth was an above-average fielder, and Gehrig was transformed under Huggins from a gangly, awkward kid into a sure-handed gloveman. "People forget that the Yankees in the twenties were more than a great offensive club," said Yankee pitcher Sam Jones. "They were the best *defensive* team in both leagues, as well. That outfield, terrific pitching, a great infield. It was a well-balanced ball club, in every way."[7]

Ironically, the one Yankee closest to Huggins' heart was a weak-hitting rookie who later starred for the Cardinals and himself became a great manager by imitating his strategies, although not his quiet manner. "I was training myself to become a manager even then," said Leo Durocher, a shortstop in 1928. "I kept a little black book in my pocket, and when I wasn't playing I would sit beside Mr. Huggins and write down every move he made. At night, I would study the more interesting situations that had come up, and then I'd give myself a test by writing and rewriting exactly what he had done and what the thinking had been behind it.

"Not that I ever discussed strategy with him," continued Durocher, who called Huggins a master of basic psychology. "Miller Huggins was not a talkative man."[8]

But even as the Yankees won, Huggins' health deteriorated. A boil on his cheek grew red and angry until it threatened his vision, but rather than seek medical treatment, Huggins repaired to the trainer's room to sit under a sunlamp—a popular (and vastly overrated) treatment for many ailments in the twenties.

"Take over the reins today," Huggins told Arthur Fletcher, his third base coach. "I'll be back tomorrow."

While he was baking under the lamp, the manager heard Waite Hoyt storm into the clubhouse. "What happened to you?" he demanded.

"I was knocked out of the box," admitted Hoyt. "Joe Hauser hit a home run off me. I don't know how. I could always handle that guy, pitching him high."

"How old are you, Waite?"

"I was thirty last week."

"Well, you have to make up your mind you can't do after thirty all the things you used to do. You don't bounce back the way you did. You have to spare your strength and get more rest."[9]

Ironically, Huggins could have used this bit of advice himself. The boil overtook the eye, and despite frequent blood transfusions, the forty-nine-year-old manager died of erysipelas ten days later, on September 25, 1929. A game was in progress when the Yankees received the news, and several burst into tears, bawling unashamedly in the dugout. Babe Ruth, the major cause of the manager's troubles over the years, wept the most. "He was a great guy, was Hug," said Ruth, adding a tribute that should have appeared on the manager's tombstone. "He was a tough little guy, and the only one who knew how to handle me."

Huggins's overall managerial record showed 1,413 wins and 1,134 losses for a .555 winning percentage. The Mighty Mite was elected to the Hall of Fame in 1964.

Adrian Constantine "Cap" Anson

Cornelius "Connie" Alexander Mack (nee McGillicuddy) with rookie pitchers Bob Shantz, Clement Hausmann, and Jimmie Wilson

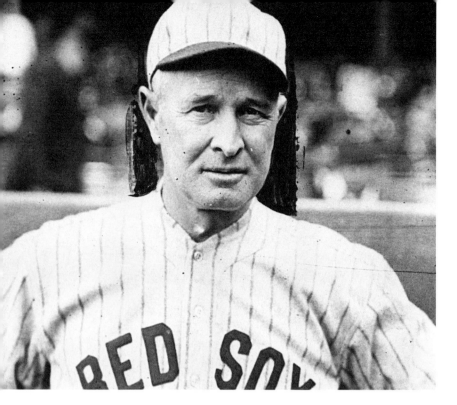

Frank Leroy Chance

John Joseph McGraw

Miller James Huggins

Joseph Vincent McCarthy

Charles "Casey" Dillon Stengel

Leo Ernest Durocher

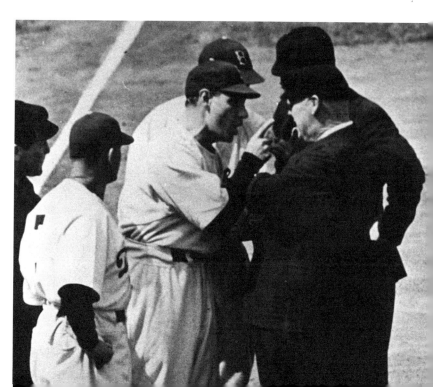

Walter Emmons Alston

Earl Sidney Weaver

*George "Sparky" Anderson
(left) talks with Dave Concepcion*

Dorrel Norman Elvert "Whitey" Herzog

6 ◇ JOE McCARTHY: THE PUSHBUTTON MANAGER

During the 1938 season, while three young New York pitchers were all but snoozing in the New York dugout during batting practice, Yankee hurling ace Red Ruffing raced around the outfield trying to catch fly balls. Because of a mining accident in his youth that had cost him four toes on his left foot, Ruffing had to hustle to snag balls that swifter fielders easily caught. Despite his handicap, however, this future Hall-of-Famer was playing in the third straight season in which he won twenty or more games.

Yankee manager Joe McCarthy's flinty brown eyes switched from Ruffing to the trio of loafers. Every pitcher on the Yankees knew the manager's theory that a pitcher's arm is no stronger than his legs.

"Somebody tell that Ruffing to quit working so hard," barked McCarthy. "The way he's going he won't last another ten years in the big leagues."[1]

The three young pitchers hastily located their gloves and sprinted to the outfield. When Joe McCarthy talked, you listened or you were gone. "McCarthy probably would laugh in your face if you told him he was a psychologist, but he was, one of the shrewdest in his handling of ballplayers of any manager who ever lived," said writer Tom Meany in *The Yankee Story* (1960). "McCarthy was a practicing psychologist and didn't know it."

Partly because of his intensity, Joe McCarthy ranked as one of the best managers ever to stalk a dugout. "When McCarthy became angry, there was always the feeling that not only jobs or careers were at stake, but also arms, legs, jaws and possibly life itself," said *Rochester Democrat and Chronicle* feature writer Curt Smith.[2] In twenty-four years as a skipper, he always finished in the first division, and he won pennants in both the American League and the National League—the first manager to accomplish that feat. In World Series play, his teams won twenty-nine games against only nine defeats. His major-league winning percentage of .614 was the best in history, as was his record of achieving six one-hundred-win seasons in his managing career.

Curiously, this man who became one of baseball's best known—although not best loved—managers, was unknown outside bush-league baseball until he was nearly forty. Joseph Vincent McCarthy was born on April 21, 1887, in that section of Philadelphia, Pennsylvania, that was called Germantown. As a teenager he lost his father, a contractor, in a construction accident, and the youth labored for $6.50 a week in a textile factory to help his mother. Whenever he had spare change, he bought tickets to watch Connie Mack manage the Athletics. His devotion to the old manager was so great that he even used to walk reverentially behind Mack from the ballpark to the streetcar after A's ballgames. McCarthy also loved to play sandlot ball and was a standout despite his relatively small 5'8", 170-pound frame. "Give a boy a bat and a ball and a place to play and you'll have a good citizen," said McCarthy later, recalling how the game had affected his life for the better. Unfortunately, a broken kneecap he suffered in a boyhood game slowed him enough to keep him from ever reaching the major leagues as a player.

His first break came while playing baseball on a scholarship for Niagara University, a Catholic college north of Buffalo, New York. A representative of Wilmington of the Tri-State League saw him play and offered him a contract in 1907. He dropped out of school without completing his sophomore year. Curiously, he played only a dozen games for Wilmington when a better offer came from Franklin, Pennsylvania, in the old Interstate League. Like other ballplayers of his era, the youngster's bonus for signing with Franklin was not lucrative. "They gave me a bus ticket to get down there and that was about it."[3]

McCarthy's first season gave him the false hope that someday he might play in the big leagues. The right-handed batter hit .314 in seventy-one games for Franklin and was rated a steady glove man at second, third, and short. But although he consistently batted more than .250 in the high minors in stints with Toledo of the American Association, Wilkes-Barre of the New York State League, and Buffalo of the International League, no major-league team invited him to spring training until 1916. Reports on McCarthy said that his bad knee hampered his speed. "If it weren't for that knee we'd recommend you," several major-league scouts informed him. His best year was 1913, when Wilkes-Barre named him its player-manager. McCarthy not only guided the club to a second-place finish, he batted a career-high .325, including fifty-one extra base hits in 132 games.

In 1916, though, the aging busher finally thought he'd get an opportunity to ascend to the majors. Both the New York Yankees and Brooklyn of the upstart Federal League offered him contracts. Believing his best chance of success was with the weaker team, he signed with Brooklyn. To his frustration the league folded before he ever played a game. He returned to exile in the high minors with Louisville of the American Association.

Three years later, the Louisville manager was fired during the 1919 season, and McCarthy became its player-manager, piloting the team to a third-place finish. In 1920 the team finished second. In 1921, his last year as a player, McCarthy's club captured the American Association pennant with a 98–70 record, then repeated in 1925.

Up to this time, owners of major-league teams mainly considered players with big-league experience for managing positions in the American and National leagues. But word of McCarthy's 102 wins during the 1925 season at Louisville reached William Wrigley, owner of the Chicago Cubs, who signed the thirty-nine-year-old bush-league genius. "You know, when I went to manage the Cubs in 1926, I took over a team that had finished last the year before," recalled McCarthy. "Well, some of my friends in Germantown gave me a dinner before I left for spring training, sort of to wish me luck. Connie [Mack] was invited. When I got up to make my few remarks, I said . . . I hoped to have the pleasure sometime of meeting him in a World Series. Everybody laughed—they thought that was funny."[4]

But McCarthy had the last laugh. Once installed in Chicago, he boldly revamped the team, even dropping future Hall-of-Famer Grover Cleveland Alexander because the hard-drinking pitcher was uncooperative. "I had to get rid of him," McCarthy told Donald Honig, author of *The Man in the Dugout* (1977). "He didn't obey orders. A fellow asked me one time if Alex followed the rules. 'Sure he did,' I said, 'but they were always Alex's rules.' "

McCarthy guided the lowly Cubs to four straight first-division finishes, culminating in a Chicago pennant in 1929. His most valuable player was Hack Wilson, whom he plucked out of the New York Giants' farm system because manager John McGraw forgot to recall Wilson from the minors as league rules required. Taken on a technicality by the vigilant McCarthy, Wilson blossomed as a player, hitting as many as 56 homers and knocking in 190 runs in a single season.

The American League's top team in 1929 was Mack's Philadelphia. But a storybook ending was not to be. The Cubs lost the World Series in five games. In 1930, Chicago was in second place when Wrigley shocked the baseball world by forcing the best manager in the game to resign under pressure.

"The chewing gum king didn't realize it, but when he fired the busher who had made him his first million dollars in baseball and brought the Cubs back to a pre-eminent position in Chicago's bitter baseball rivalry, he kicked him upstairs," wrote Joe Williams in *The Saturday Evening Post*. The New York Yankees snatched up McCarthy, and in just two years he led them to a pennant and a World Series triumph over Wrigley's Cubs.

The McCarthy era was a thrilling time for Yankee fans. He brought seven world championships and eight titles to New York from 1931 to 1946. Many years his teams crushed the opposition. The 1936 world title was won by 19½ games over Boston, at that time the largest margin of victory ever by an American League team. McCarthy's 1937 Bronx Bombers finished first by thirteen games over Boston, and his 1939 Yanks were seventeen games ahead of the second-place Red Sox.

Seldom was a manager so devoted to strategy as Joe McCarthy. In those pre-computer days the manager had no statistics to tell him how to assess enemy batters and pitchers. Instead, he memorized box scores and always knew who was hot and who was not. He'd walk a .200 banjo hitter if the man had hit well in his last couple of games to pitch to a .300 hitter who had been in a slump. Quite often he was the first to discover when the so-called book on hitters was incorrect. For several games the Yankee pitchers fed high balls to Roger Cramer and Mule Haas of the Athletics, because that was the pitch other teams were throwing them. But when Cramer and Haas connected one time too many, McCarthy wised up. "We have been just plain dumb," he told his pitchers. "It's the low one inside those guys can't hit."[5]

McCarthy was a tactical genius, contrary to nay-sayers who believed that even a fan off the street could win with the talent he had in New York. When the Yankees faced fastballing southpaw Lefty Grove of the Philadelphia Athletics, the manager went against baseball logic by writing a lineup that was dominated by left-handed batters. Knowing that right-handers would try to pull Grove, out of pride and habit, McCarthy used left-handed batters, who slapped his smoking pitches to the opposite field, thereby improving their chances of reaching base safely.

McCarthy's success as a New York manager was partially due to his insistence on matching his strategy to his team's strengths. Realizing that the Yankees were a power club, he never took the bat out of slugging Lou Gehrig's hands by asking him to sacrifice runners along, as John McGraw would have done. "I never asked Gehrig to bunt, not once in eight years," said McCarthy. "I don't think that would have been very good strategy." Nor did he ask the fleet Joe DiMaggio to steal except in crucial situations, not wanting to risk the center fielder's tender knees for short-term gains. He also played his best players day-in and day-out, even if they had minor injuries, helping Gehrig achieve his incredible streak of appearing in 2,130 straight games.

One reason that McCarthy won is that he never made wholesale changes with his club. As soon as he recognized that a man could no longer play his position, the manager made a change. He knew that if he waited too long to find a replacement, two or three positions might grow weak, and his once-strong team might collapse. "You have to improve your club if it means letting your own brother go," McCarthy told Ed Fitzgerald of *Sport* magazine in 1973.

When he needed reinforcements, he often plucked talented players from the Yankee farm system and made them fit into new positions, rather than have them languish on the bench behind established stars. McCarthy was always a teacher. "When you know in your heart you've helped some of these young fellows make good, when you know you've played a part in their success, that's when you know you're accomplishing something—you're not wasting your time," he informed *Sport*'s Fitzgerald. When the great second baseman Tony Lazzeri began to slip, McCarthy took a shortstop prospect named Joe Gordon and converted him into a future MVP second sacker. When a kid shortstop named Red Rolfe lacked the arm to throw out runners from the hole in 1934, the manager helped the future .289 career hitter adjust to third base. "He broke in at third up at Fenway Park," McCarthy told sportswriter Donald Honig. "The first ball hit down to him took a bad bounce and hit him in the eye and blackened it. He came into the dugout holding his eye and said, 'Joe, you gave me some bad information.' But he became a good third baseman."

The manager was a stickler for fundamentals and never let mental errors go unnoticed on the field, although he accepted dropped balls and other physical errors as part of the game. Because McCarthy emphasized alertness and how to think several plays ahead, the Yankees learned not to beat themselves.

McCarthy had pet theories that served him well. He believed that all good managers had three things in common: a good memory, patience, and the ability to recognize and utilize talent. Moreover, he always tried to have the best double play combination in baseball, believing that there was no better way to get out of a troubled inning. His second maxim was that all pitchers needed to learn how to field. He considered pitchers with good gloves such as Red Ruffing to be fifth infielders.[6]

McCarthy knew how to make the best use of talent available to him. He helped beetle-browed Charlie "King Kong" Keller develop into a power hitter, saving him from becoming just another journeyman outfielder. The left-handed spray hitter managed to hit just eleven home runs in his rookie season of 1939, but McCarthy realized that many of Keller's best pokes were caught in the spacious confines of left and center fields in Yankee Stadium.

"Why do you think they built such a short right field in this ball park?" McCarthy demanded.

"For Ruth," replied Keller.

"That's right. So why aren't you taking advantage of it? You're a left-handed power hitter."

McCarthy knew it wouldn't be easy for the youngster to switch his batting style. If the move wasn't done just right, the youngster's performance would slip and his confidence would erode. The manager, without Keller's knowledge, ordered his batting practice pitchers to throw inside pitches to him, forcing the youth to get the head of the bat around quickly. Soon, as batting practice pitches began descending like hailstones off Keller's bat into the right-field bleachers, the lefty gained enough confidence to pull the ball in game situations. In 1940 he hit twenty-one home runs and then belted thirty-one a year later. "That's how we got him used to doing it," admitted McCarthy. "So you see, there are a lot of things managers never talk about that people think just happen. But things don't just happen. I don't want to sound like I'm bragging. I'm just explaining the way things work."[7]

McCarthy's career-long problem was in overcoming a nickname that was inadvertently given to him by Jimmy Dykes, then the manager of the Chicago White Sox. Dykes had wisecracked to a reporter that he thought McCarthy was only "a pushbutton manager" who had better players on the bench than most managers had starting. "When I said that, I had no intention of casting any reflections on his ability," said a contrite Dykes. "He was a good manager; he had to be or he wouldn't have been winning as often as he did. . . . I never meant to be critical of Joe."[8]

Nonetheless, the label stuck, as did the sobriquet of "Marse Joe," a name that implied a stern, domineering manager who treated his players like slaves. To be sure, McCarthy demanded that his players always look like champions on and off the field. He had personal prejudices, making players wear ties and condemning card playing, beer drinking, and pipe smoking, even though he himself drank whiskey and smoked cigars.

Many Yankee ballplayers disliked the demanding McCarthy, but they respected his record and dedication. Babe Ruth, the slugger who was over the hill when he played for McCarthy, resented the skipper because the Bambino had hoped to become Yankee manager himself. Nonetheless, he respected the manager too much to mutiny, as he'd done years before against former New York manager Miller Huggins. McCarthy's worst enemy was hard-partying relief pitcher Joe Page, but even Page admired the former busher. "I hated his guts, but there was never a better manager," said Page. Other Bronx Bombers such as Lou Gehrig and Joe DiMaggio thought McCarthy was the salt of the earth and seldom argued with him.

McCarthy showed his most unpleasant side while haranguing umpires. But although he argued with them, he always stopped short of pushing them to the point where they threw him out of games. He knew that it was difficult to devise a strategy from the clubhouse stool, and so he always remained in control of his emotions, even when he disputed a decision.

By the end of World War II, "Marse Joe" had grown disenchanted with the Yankees. He hated the patchwork ballclubs he managed during the war while his regulars were in military service, and his authority was challenged by the new owners, Larry MacPhail, Dan Topping, and Del Webb. He quit the Yankees during the 1946 season, when his team dropped to third, seventeen games behind league-leading Boston. But in 1948, he signed a contract to manage his old enemy, the Red Sox, led by tempermental slugger Ted Williams. Knowing that Williams had screamed for years that no one would make him wear a tie, McCarthy defused a possible confrontation by beginning to wear shirts with open collars.

McCarthy managed brilliantly that year, making the right moves on the diamond to compensate for a pitching staff that lacked a single twenty-game winner. But despite his magic, the season ended in a tie with Cleveland for the American League pennant, and a one-game playoff decided the winner. Perhaps recalling how a washed-up pitcher named Howard Ehmke of the Philadelphia A's had beaten his Cubs in the opening game of the 1929 World Series, McCarthy started a fading second-line pitcher named Denny Galehouse, who was in his last full season in the majors. "We were in a close race all the way, and my starters were all used up from getting us into the playoff," said McCarthy. "And Galehouse had pitched a great game for me against the Indians the last time we were in Cleveland. I was hoping he would do it again, but he didn't, and we lost [8–3]. What the hell, I could have started [Mel] Parnell or [Ellis] Kinder or one of the others, but then I would have been second-guessed for starting a tired pitcher. No matter what you do, you get second-guessed."[9]

The 1949 season involved another cliffhanger finish, this time between Boston and McCarthy's former Yankees. But once again McCarthy came up one game short, and his critics accused him of blowing the pennant. Ill and unanxious to return, he retired from baseball to his farm outside of Buffalo, New York, with his wife Elizabeth. There he was content to be known by locals as "the Squire of Ellicott Creek."

Growing mellower in his old age, McCarthy became a favorite of young reporters looking for a bit of nostalgia. His famed memory remained sharp until the end. When asked by Curt Smith who his most cherished ballplayer had been, the man who managed Babe Ruth, Ted Williams, and Joe DiMaggio didn't hesitate to respond. "Lou

Gehrig was a man who came through in the clutch for you above all others," said McCarthy. "When we needed a lift, you'd look to him, and he seldom failed you."

In 1957, twenty years before his death at ninety from pneumonia, the one-time busher was admitted into the Hall of Fame. Even though he was an old man, the public still idolized him. "I get mail from all over the country . . . a lot of them from kids," McCarthy told Donald Honig. "One kid, he wrote and said he's nine years old and has been a fan of mine all his life. Can you imagine that? All his life?"

7 CASEY STENGEL: THE OLD PROFESSOR

Charles Dillon Stengel was born on July 30, 1890, in Kansas City, Missouri. Eventually, though, he would receive the nickname of "KC"—the slang word for his hometown—which sportswriters would spell as "Casey."

Young Stengel was the paternal grandson of a German immigrant, and his mother's mother came from famine-struck Ireland. Jennie, his mother, doted upon him, perhaps because he was the youngest of three children. Stengel's brother was a speedy all-around athlete named Grant who, ironically, was thought to be the one who would go far in baseball. None of the other neighborhood children wanted to choose the jug-eared, bowlegged Charles—then called "Dutch"—to play with them in pickup games, but Grant refused to play unless his kid brother were also selected. The two would do anything to win, even substituting a potato for the baseball with a man on base, to work an illegal version of the hidden-ball play.

Stengel was never an outstanding student, perhaps partly because Mrs. Kennedy, one of his earliest teachers, insisted that the left-handed youngster needed to learn how to write with his right hand. "I don't blame Mrs. Kennedy for making me change over," he later charitably said. "When I got into baseball I thought it was a great thing that she made me write right-handed because I became a good fielder after being an awkward kid because I could use my right hand better. I stayed left-handed in throwing and hitting, but in catching the ball I naturally had to use my right hand, and because of my penmanship I was more agile with my right hand than any person who had stayed left-handed."[1]

Stengel attended Central High School and played varsity baseball under William Driver, later a coach at the University of Mississippi. After high school, Stengel decided to become a dentist, attending Western Dental College in his hometown. Stengel's college career was marked more by his love of pranks than his love of studying. He once put a lit cigar in the mouth of a corpse used for anatomy classes, and he covered himself with a white sheet and lay down on a slab to scare the daylights out of his classmates by rising slowly when they bent over the supposedly dead body.[2] Also, his studies frustrated him, mainly because all dental equipment in those days was made for right-handed users, and when he was given an opportunity to play professional baseball, he left the dental profession without regret.

Stengel had evolved into a decent ballplayer as his body matured and reached its full 5'11", 175-pound size. But back then he thought he might become known for his pitching prowess. For $1 a day, he played for a barnstorming semipro team called the Kansas City Red Sox, which traveled occasionally to distant Wyoming and Utah to play games. His reputation as a strong-armed hurler reached the Kansas City Blues of the American Association, who scouted the lad and liked what they saw, signing him to a $135-a-month contract for the 1910 season.

Before reporting to spring training, Stengel decided to seek the advice of a famous neighbor, Charles (Kid)

Nichols, then the winningest pitcher in National League history with 362 victories. "Listen to your manager," said Nichols. "Or if you have an old player teaching you, listen to him. Never say, 'I won't do that.' Always listen. If you're not going to do what he says, don't tell him so. Let it go in one ear, and let it roll around in there for a month, and then if it isn't any good let it go out the other ear. But if it is *good*, memorize it and keep it. You do that and you'll learn something, and you'll keep out of a lot of trouble."[3]

Ironically, Stengel disregarded much of Nichols' advice. Before his playing career ended, he had gained a reputation as a troublemaker and baseball clown. Stengel switched from pitching to the outfield and was purchased by Brooklyn in 1912. He debuted on September twelfth of that same year and made headlines in his first game, collecting four hits in four trips to the plate and finishing the month with a .316 batting average. During his first full season in 1913, the twenty-two-year-old batted a respectable .272, with seven home runs and forty-three RBIs. In the off-season he helped his former coach, William Driver, direct the baseball team at the University of Mississippi. He talked so much about his college exploits to Brooklyn teammates that they called him "Professor," a nickname that seemed particularly appropriate in his later years.

In 1914, Stengel looked like a shoo-in for stardom. He batted .316 for Brooklyn manager Wilbert Robinson, but he somehow never seemed to reach the potential others predicted for him. For one thing, he seemed to have difficulty concentrating, except for late-season "must" games and during postseason play. His penchant for pranks and late-night escapades matched those of his teammates, and the club gained the dubious nickname of the Daffyness Boys. In spite of its zany roster, Brooklyn won a pennant in 1916, and Stengel batted .364 against Babe Ruth's Bostonians in a five-game World Series won by the Red Sox.

After the 1917 season, Stengel became a journeyman player, joining Pittsburgh in 1918 and playing only two months before enlisting in the navy to participate in the tail-end of World War I. In 1919 the Phillies bought him, but he refused to report until the following year because of a contract dispute, gaining him a reputation as something of a malcontent in those pre-free–agency days.

In 1921, the Giants picked him up in a multiplayer trade, and Stengel had the opportunity to study the game under legendary manager John McGraw, who led New York to pennants in 1922 and 1923. The outfielder played his best baseball under World Series pressure, ending up with a .393 average for twelve games.

Stengel's knock-kneed running style, his jumbo ears, and his prematurely wrinkled skin made him a favorite among sportswriters. Ring Lardner based a fictional character on him in "Alibi Ike," and Damon Runyan wrote a wonderful story on Stengel's inside-the-park home run during Game One of the 1923 Giants-Yankees World Series, the first ever scheduled in the new Yankee Stadium.

With two outs in the ninth, the score tied at four apiece, Stengel stroked an opposite-field drive off pitcher Joe Bush to deep left center. While New York outfielders Bob Meusel and Whitey Witt ran like rabbits after the ball, the aging Stengel wheezed painfully around the bases. A bruised heel and a slipping rubber pad over the bruise slowed him down even further, and his run around the bases was a torturous event for Giant fans to witness. Runyan's account in the New York *American* on October 10, 1923, is a masterpiece.

> *This is the way old Casey Stengel ran yesterday afternoon running his home run home to a Giant victory by a score of 5 to 4 in the first game of the World Series of 1923.*
> *This is the way old Casey Stengel ran running his home run home when two were out in the ninth inning and the score was tied, and the ball still bounding inside the Yankee yard.*
> *This is the way—*

His mouth wide open.

His warped old legs bending beneath him at every stride.

His arms flying back and forth like those of a man swimming with a crawl stroke.

His flanks heaving, his breath whistling, his head far back. Yankee infielders, passed by Old Casey Stengel as he was running his home run home, say Casey was muttering to himself, adjuring himself to greater speed as a jockey mutters to his horse in a race, saying "go on, Casey, go on."

The warped old legs, twisted and bent by many a year of baseball campaigning, just barely held out under Casey until he reached the plate, running his home run home.

Then they collapsed.

Stengel ended his career with the Boston Braves in 1925. He wound up with a respectable .284 career batting average. But what fans recalled most about him was his flair for the ridiculous. Had he never managed a day, Stengel's place in baseball lore was assured by his exploits on the playing field. Batting against the Pirates at Ebbets Field in his first game against Brooklyn in an enemy uniform, Stengel called for time and doffed his cap to acknowledge the boos of his former fans. To the surprise of the ballpark, a sparrow hidden inside the hat flew out.

While with New York, his after-hours habits became so irritating to the Giants' management that manager John McGraw assigned a detective to watch Stengel and other players. According to legend, Stengel was miffed when he found out that one detective had been assigned to follow both teammate Irish Meusel and him. "I thought I deserved my own," he complained.[4]

But his after-hours carousing came to a halt after he met Edna Lawson, heiress to a housing and banking fortune, and married her on August 16, 1924. "If you're going to print anything about us, you can say for the bridegroom that it is the best catch he ever made in his career," Stengel told reporters after the wedding.

Stengel—although continuing to delight in playing the clown around sportswriters—could be as serious as an FBI agent after he became manager of the Brooklyn Dodgers in 1934. He was particularly serious when it came to teaching baseball fundamentals. Never trusting to luck, he insisted that a pitcher never throw the ball until all his fielders were properly positioned and that every pitched ball should go to a particular spot, thereby diminishing a batter's chances of hitting a long ball or cleaning the bases with a line drive to left or right. Stengel's Yankee aces such as Whitey Ford—named to the Hall of Fame in 1974—always threw to spots instead of collecting strikeouts. "Throw those sinkers," he advised his pitchers. "Make 'em hit ground balls. Never heard anyone gettin' home runs on ground balls."[5] Likewise, he urged his batters to simply meet the ball, knowing that overswinging leads to prolonged slumps and multiple strikeouts. "Hit him easy—not too hard, not too soft—the ball'll move," commanded Stengel. "Otherwise you're a strikeout king, not a home run king."[6]

Until his late fifties, when he received the opportunity to manage the world-class New York Yankees, Stengel regarded his career as a manager as a terrible failure. He managed the Brooklyn Dodgers from 1934 to 1936 and had such a dreadful record that the club fired him right before the 1937 season began, even though they had already paid him. From 1938 to 1943, he managed the lifeless Boston Braves, again without success. Not once with those two clubs did Stengel so much as bring a club into the first division, and only once (1938) did he manage a club that played at least .500 baseball. Sportswriters thought little of him as a field general. In fact, when a taxi hit Stengel, breaking his leg and sidelining him for two months, a Boston reporter suggested that the cab driver win a trophy as "The Man Who Did the Most for Baseball in 1943."[7]

Stengel admittedly made mistakes during his early years as a manager. One of his worst decisions was to ship Warren Spahn back to Boston's minor leagues in 1942, after failing to recognize the genius of the Buffalo-born southpaw who was destined to win 363 games in his big-league career, passing Kid Nichols' old record. Ironically, when Stengel's career wound down with the Mets in 1965, he signed the forty-four-year-old Spahn. "I knew Casey before and after he was a genius," joked Spahn.

But Stengel was a strategist even during his woeful years in Brooklyn and Boston, although his moves were wasted on players who consistently failed to perform up to his demanding standards. One strategy that he cooked up with the Dodgers was a pickoff play with a man on third. The pitcher was to throw the ball at the batter's head, screaming "Look out!" even as he released the pitch. As Stengel imagined the play, the batter would duck or hit the dirt, the runner on third would stand paralyzed, and the catcher would throw the ball to the third baseman for the easy tag. Unfortunately, Stengel once recalled, not only did the man on base freeze, but so did the Brooklyn third baseman. After several balls wound up in the left-field corner, an unhappy Stengel discontinued the play.[8]

Stengel knocked around the minor leagues as a manager, winning pennants in three Triple A cities. Finally, following the 1948 baseball season, he obtained the break of his life when new Yankee owners Dan Topping and George Weiss paid him $35,000 a year to replace former New York manager Bucky Harris, whom they blamed for taking a preseason pennant favorite to a disappointing third-place finish. Because Topping and Weiss had criticized Harris for being too lax with players, Casey Stengel led the Yankees through a very physically demanding spring training session in 1949, telling the players that "most games are lost, not won."

"I've been hired to win, and I think I will," he told reporters. "There is less wrong with the Yankees than any club I've ever had."[9]

But Stengel's critics lambasted the decision to hire him. They made fun of his rambling style of talking, labeling it "Stengelese." "The Yankees have now been mathematically eliminated from the 1949 pennant race," wrote Dave Egan in the Boston *Record*. "They eliminated themselves when they engaged Perfesser Casey Stengel to mismanage them for the next two years."

Indeed, few pollsters thought the Yankees had any chance of regaining the winning form they had demonstrated under managers Miller Huggins and Joe McCarthy. Ironically, several players had bad reputations as horse-race gamblers and midnight carousers. The Yankees even had several men shadowed by private detectives, but Stengel stopped Weiss from trading the players, insisting he could handle troublemakers. "You can tear a team apart in a couple of weeks," reasoned Stengel, "but it takes years to put one back together again."[10]

Stengel managed the club, generally expected to finish fourth at best, to a pennant in his first season, despite a serious heel injury to Joe DiMaggio, one of seventy-one injuries the Yankees incurred in 1949. Even the trainer, Gus Mauch, broke a rib when he walked into a parking meter.

The manager ignored the media's insistence that one-time stalwart Yankees such as Phil Rizzuto, Tommy Henrich, Charlie (King Kong) Keller, and Johnny Lindell were past their prime, drawing respectable years out of his veterans by wisely platooning them. In the mid-fifties, critics often accused Stengel of being a pushbutton manager, but in 1949 he overcame serious weaknesses behind the plate and in the infield by bringing up and developing such promising youngsters as Hank Bauer, Gene Woodling, Yogi Berra, Jerry Coleman, and Bobby Brown. Stengel managed masterfully, winning twenty-eight games by one run. The 1949 season came down to the last two games of the season, and the Yankees overcame a one-game Boston lead by defeating Joe McCarthy's Red Sox by 5–4 and 5–3 margins. Then, silencing his enemies forever, the old Professor led his troops to a five-game World Series triumph over Brooklyn.

"I've been on a lot of pennant teams, but I'll never forget this one," said Joe DiMaggio, who was allowed by Stengel to tell him on what days he was well enough to play. "What did we have? Not a single man hitting in 100 runs. Not a regular hitting .300, and they can't count me because I was out half a season [DiMaggio hit .346 in a mere 76 games]. One twenty-game pitcher [Vic Raschi]. Boy, it just shows you what guts will do!"[11]

Curiously, after Stengel won the pennant, his detractors then blasted him for being too much of a strategist. "Nobody knows any more about the game," wrote *Look* magazine's Tim Cohane. "But he is too much the purist, the theorist, the strategist. He is always trying to make a player pull something he's never tried before. If the player can assimilate it, he's the better for it. If he can't, Stengel keeps needling him until finally he is useless to the team."

But in retrospect such criticism seems largely inspired by sour grapes. In 1949, Stengel became one of the first managers to realize that it was more important to win ballgames than to have his starting pitchers collect complete games. During his career, Stengel consistently developed some of the game's finest relief pitchers, including Joe Page (13–8 and twenty-seven saves in 1949) and a decade later, nearsighted Ryne Duren. "We stressed that our pitchers pitch hard to all hitters—not to pace themselves—but to leave it to our great relief pitcher, Joe Page, to finish it if they tired," Stengel told writer Charles B. Cleveland following the 1949 Series' opener, a two-hit 1–0 shutout by Reynolds won on Tommy Henrich's ninth-inning homer. To thwart the Dodgers' best hitters, Stengel pitched Jackie Robinson low and slugger Duke Snider high and tight, strategies that took the bats out of their hands.[12]

In World Series competition, when every game became a must-win, the manager had no qualms about putting starters such as Allie Reynolds into the bull pen. During the 1950 series, after the Yankees had nipped Detroit for the pennant, Stengel used Reynolds as both a starter and reliever in a four-game sweep of Philadelphia's young club, aptly named the "Whiz Kids."

Stengel won in 1950 even though he had incurred the great DiMaggio's wrath by benching him for weak hitting, as well as that of Joe Page, who thought he had been overused. The manager insisted that the players' criticisms meant nothing to him. "The secret of managing a club is to keep the five guys who hate you away from the five who are undecided."

Without question, Stengel became the manager of the decade during the fifties, winning world championships in each of his first five years with New York. Thanks to such future Hall of Famers as pitcher Whitey Ford, slugger Mickey Mantle, and catcher Yogi Berra, the Yankees became the most feared and hated team in baseball. With all those sluggers, Stengel rarely relied on steals or sacrifices to score runs, quipping that the biggest problem the Yankees had on the base paths was getting out of the way of line drives.

The manager showed particularly brilliant strategy in the way he spared Ford by pitching him in spots instead of as part of a regular rotation, never starting him in more than thirty-three games in a single season.

Stengel also won by emphasizing the importance of defense, in particular the need to turn double plays. Stengel always dumped "them fellas who drive in two runs and let in three." He liked to remind his great keystone combinations that every double play they turned was "two-twenty-sevenths of a ballgame."

Without doubt the manager's trademark was his success at platooning ballplayers. One of his more successful efforts at platooning was his decision to alternate left-handed-hitting Gene Woodling with Hank Bauer, a right-handed hitter. "You couldn't complain too much," said Bauer philosophically. "We walked into the bank every October."[13] Nonetheless, Stengel was no slave to strategy. He often threw left-handed batters against left-handed pitchers, for example, if a batter were on a hot streak. "People alter percentages," said Stengel, who could reel off on demand a list of players whose performances outweighed percentages.

In 1954, Stengel's Yankees finished second to the pitching-rich Cleveland Indians, but with 103 wins to their credit, the Bronx Bombers hardly blamed themselves. New York rebounded to win four straight pennants, including two more World Series winners' rings. The 1959 season was another off-year, finding the Yankees finishing third, but in 1960 the manager again led the club to a pennant.

Nonetheless, despite his incredible record, the Yankees failed to renew Stengel's contract after Bill Mazeroski's dramatic ninth-inning home run in the seventh game gave Pittsburgh the win and the World Series. The Yankee management felt that the loss was somehow due to the manager's age and let him go despite his ten pennants and seven world championships. Understandably, he was bitter. "I'll never make the mistake again of being seventy-years old," he said, adding philosophically some months later, "Most people my age are dead."

But Stengel had one more opportunity to manage in 1962, when he was hired by the expansion-era Mets. With the Mets he demonstrated that he still remained the consummate teacher, coming out early to the ballpark despite his seventy-odd years to drill players on fundamentals. Since he lacked the wonderful power hitters that he had always enjoyed with the Yankees, Stengel went back to playing the bunt-and-run game, which he'd learned as a young player. Even in something so simple as the basic bunt play, the Ol' Perfessor had theories about execution that his players were well advised to learn. According to Stengel, "the most effective way of bunting is to hit directly downward—he calls it chopping wood—so that (1) the catcher will be the only man around to make a play and (2) will be able only to throw out the batter at first while other runners advance."[14]

Nonetheless, the old man's magic was clearly gone. He finished dead last for three straight seasons and called it quits in 1965 after breaking his hip at age seventy-four.

Stengel's saddest trial to bear in his last years came in 1974, when his beloved Edna suffered several ravaging strokes that left her virtually helpless. "She went crazy on me overnight," he lamented to friends. "I miss her." Stengel contracted lymphatic cancer and died on September 29, 1975, at eighty-five, his own mind failing at the time of his death. Edna lingered for nearly three years after the Old Professor's passing, and when she died the press learned that the two had known as much about financial strategies as Stengel knew about baseball strategies. Their combined estate was worth $3 million.

If a list of ballplayers were compiled who regarded Casey Stengel as the greatest manager of all time, it would stretch from homeplate to centerfield. "I've been in big-league baseball for fifteen years and I thought I knew a lot about the game, but this man knows more than anyone I ever ran up against," marveled white-haired Richie Ashburn, the onetime Phillies all-star who ended his career with the ignominious early Mets.[15]

8 LEO DUROCHER: FURY ON THE FIELD

Leo Ernest Durocher managed for twenty-four years in the majors, compiling 2,019 wins versus only 1,709 losses for a .542 winning percentage. As a player, sportswriters called him "Lippy" because he sassed great players such as Babe Ruth and Ty Cobb when he broke into the bigs as a shortstop in 1928. When Durocher became a manager, writers referred to him as "The Lip," citing his feuds with team owners, players, and umpires.

Durocher's mother gave birth to him on a kitchen table on July 27, 1905, in the French-Catholic community of Springfield, Massachusetts. His father, George, worked for the Boston and Albany Railroad until a heart attack disabled him, forcing Leo's mother to work as a maid in a downtown hotel. One Christmas, the family lacked the money even to purchase a Christmas tree, but he had a happy childhood nonetheless, never lacking for necessities. To earn spending money, the boy worked as a soda jerk in an ice-cream parlor and hustled pool games.

When Leo was twelve his family opened a boarding house on Elm Street in Springfield, two blocks away from where Rabbit Maranville lived, a shortstop for the Boston Braves destined for election into the Hall of Fame. Maranville and the elder Durocher became friends, and Leo not only received his first glove from Rabbit (which Durocher used even after he reached the major leagues), but also tips which made even a boy of his frail physique a sandlot star. "Know the hitters, he would say," recalled Durocher in his autobiography, *Nice Guys Finish Last* (1975). "Study them. Anticipate where the ball was going to be hit. Get rid of the ball quick."

Maranville taught him how to cut a hole in his glove to catch the ball against bare skin for a surer—though much more painful—out. More importantly, the diminutive Maranville taught the frail youngster not to be intimidated by anyone. "Never take a backward step out there," he growled at young Durocher. "The first backward step a little man takes is the one that's going to kill him."

Though the boy listened respectfully to the major-league ballplayer's advice, few other adults could tell him anything. He punched a high school teacher and was expelled while only in the ninth grade. He went to work for an electric company and might have ended up as a blue-collar worker had he not successfully passed a two-week tryout with Hartford of the Eastern League when he was eighteen. Hartford sold Durocher to the New York Yankees in 1925, and the youngster with thinning blonde hair made the team as a brash, loudmouthed shortstop in 1928. In his first days with the champion Yankees, the rookie nearly came to blows with Detroit's immortal Ty Cobb after Durocher insulted the Georgia Peach. He snarled at teammate Babe Ruth after the slugger tried to steal cuts at Durocher's expense in batting practice.

Fortunately, on his side was New York's legendary manager Miller Huggins, another small man who identified with the spunky kid. When the young shortstop refused to be ordered from the batting cage by Babe Ruth, Huggins backed the newcomer and ordered the man who had belted sixty homers one year earlier to wait his turn.

"Never lose that self-assurance that you're the best. There are a lot of fellows around here with strong backs and weak minds," Huggins told Durocher when they were alone. "You have a strong mind and a weak back. Let them do all the hitting, you use your head. And as long as you live, there will be a place for you in baseball. You'll be here when they're all gone. . . . Little guys like us can win games. We can beat them up here," concluded Huggins, tapping his skull to emphasize the lesson.[1]

Although Durocher performed well for Huggins, hitting .270 as a rookie and fielding flawlessly while New York swept St. Louis in a four-game World Series, he was judged expendable by the Yankees when Huggins died the last week of the 1929 season. New York peddled "the All-American Out"—Babe Ruth's name for Durocher— to the dismal Cincinnati Reds after the season ended. Durocher endured three seasons with the perennial second-division team until St. Louis rescued him in a trade.

In 1933, Leo Durocher blended like an onion in stew with such roughneck Cardinals as Dizzy Dean, Joe Medwick, Frankie Frisch, and Pepper Martin. He even coined the team's famous nickname, "The Gashouse Gang." He played for the 1934 Cardinals' team that defeated Detroit for the world championship in seven games, and his reward in 1935 was to be named captain of the team. Always considered the best-fielding shortstop of his time, he nonetheless had a cumulative batting average of .333 in All-Star competition.

In October of 1937, the Brooklyn Dodgers traded four players to St. Louis for Durocher, and in spring training, manager Burleigh ("Ol' Stubblebeard") Grimes named the newcomer his team captain. But not even Durocher could spark the woeful Bums, and with three weeks left in the season Grimes was told by general manager Larry MacPhail that his contract wouldn't be renewed. MacPhail asked Grimes if he had a successor in mind.

"Yes," said Grimes, a former Giants' pitcher whose 270 wins put him into the Hall of Fame. "I think I do. You've got a guy right on the club now who's pretty smart, has got a lot of guts, and ought to be a damned good manager. . . . Durocher."[2]

At thirty-three, Leo Durocher became the player-manager of the Brooklyn Dodgers, about to scream, curse, spit—but most importantly, win—his way to base-ball glory. In that era, player-managers were common. Gabby Hartnett was one with the Cubs. Washington briefly had so-called boy manager Joe Cronin, and catcher Mickey Cochrane managed Detroit. Durocher always maintained that managing from the playing field was easier than managing from the bench.

"The two things a manager does when his team is on the field are move players and decide when to take the pitcher out," explained Durocher. "It's much easier to move a player when you're right in the middle of it, and you also have a far better sense of when your pitcher is beginning to lose it.

"The only other thing I like to do is call a pitch, *one pitch*, in a clutch situation, maybe ten or twelve times over a season. . . . When you're on the bench you have to call to the catcher to look over. When I was playing shortstop, he was looking right at me. If I left my glove open, I wanted a certain pitch. Direct communication. When the team is at bat, you're in the dugout anyway, except when you're on base, leading the club by example. Is that so bad?"[3]

Durocher tolerated neither shoddy play nor poor discipline during the 1939 season. "I'm no Simon Legree—I'm still 'Leo' to you, and still your shortstop," Durocher, a non-drinker, told the team in Clearwater before the first spring practice. "Now, about training rules: You can drink all the beer you want before the first exhibition game— at fifty bucks a glass."[4]

Durocher drove the Dodgers like a wild man all season, but he saw an immediate improvement in the heretofore horrible Bums. The 1939 team finished in third place behind the rejuvenated Cincinnati Reds, and Durocher earned the *Sporting News'* Manager of the Year award.

In 1940 Durocher brought the Dodgers in second, and again the famous cry, "Wait 'til next year," resounded in Ebbets Field. But 1941 proved to be Brooklyn's year, as The Lip guided the club to a 100–54 first-place finish behind the hustling of such youngsters as Pee Wee Reese and Pete Reiser, both only twenty-two. "Those kids, Reese and Reiser, idolized Leo and played their hearts out for him," recalled Billy Herman, a .291 hitter for the 1941 Dodgers. "And you'd be surprised how many guys there were who hated Leo's guts but who still went out there and broke their necks for him because they respected his baseball know-how."[5]

Not even the fact that the Dodgers lost the series in five games to Durocher's former club, the Yankees, was enough to dim the manager's pride in knowing he'd garnered the first pennant flag Brooklyn had been able to wave in twenty-one years.

Durocher's lack of education, which was to prove an obstacle in managing ballplayers late in his career, only helped him better understand and motivate the Dodgers who, to a man, had a lunch-bucket mentality. They prided themselves on their ability to steal enemy signs, jockey other players and umpires from the bench, intimidate batters with high, hard ones, and play hardnosed baseball on the base paths. Durocher drove the team mercilessly, setting himself up as a latter-day feudal lord, but his Brooklyn team responded. On the field he provided his youngsters with a role model, telling reporters he'd knock down his own mother if she got in his way while he tried to score.

"I might go over afterward and pick her up and say, 'Mom, I'm sorry'—but she'd still go down." On one occasion he pinch-hit a drag bunt past a Cubs pitcher in the ninth to score a man from third with the winning run.[6]

"I was traded to Brooklyn in 1943. Durocher was managing there then—best manager I ever played for," said Bobby Bragan who later managed three big-league clubs. "Never heard a ballplayer second-guess him. He never missed a move. On most teams there will be a game now and then when you hear a player say, 'I sure wish we'd have bunted that man over,' or a similar comment. I never heard those remarks when Durocher was managing. Not once. His players had implicit faith in his moves and maneuvers on the field.

"Leo had an aggressive personality. He wanted to win. That came first with him, ahead of everything else. Not everybody cottoned to him. He could irritate some people. You either loved him or you didn't; there wasn't any in-between. But by and large they all respected him."[7]

Durocher tried to retire as an active player in 1942, a disappointing year for Brooklyn supporters who saw the team win 104 games and still finish two games behind the Cardinals and their rookie phenom, Stan ("The Man") Musial. But the wartime shortage of ballplayers (Durocher being exempt because of a punctured eardrum) caused the manager to activate himself on a part-time basis in 1943 and 1945.

In 1946 the Cardinals again spoiled the Dodgers' bid for a world championship, defeating Brooklyn in a three-game playoff to break a dead-heat finish. Playing without their best player, Pete Reiser, who had broken an ankle three weeks before the season ended, the Dodgers lost to the Redbirds, bitterly disappointing Durocher and fans of "Dem Bums."

The 1947 season was a washout for Durocher. The *New York Times* on April 10, 1947, announced that Baseball Commissioner Happy Chandler had taken "the most drastic action ever taken against a major league baseball pilot." Chandler suspended Durocher for one season purportedly because the manager had publicly accused Yankee president Larry MacPhail of consorting with gamblers, but also because Durocher had been involved in a series of bad scrapes. He was engaged to marry his third wife, actress Larraine Day, who was involved at the time in a messy divorce case. He'd engaged in some notorious rhubarbs with umpires and had dared kick dirt on their shoes and even had hit one with a wet towel. Also, there were longstanding allegations that the manager himself consorted with shady characters.

The year's layoff hurt him. He had finally reached a point in his career when baseball experts universally respected him as a strategist. *Time* magazine (April 14, 1947) said "Durocher has immense ability. . . . As a tactician he is unsurpassed. . . . He has an instinct for knowing just what his players can do in any situation. He yanks pitchers quicker than any other manager and the results usually bear out his judgment."

Indeed, only the last-place Giants' pitching staff had fewer complete games than Durocher's Dodgers. Because of the heroics of Brooklyn reliever Hugh Casey (11–5, 1.98 ERA), the days when pitchers routinely threw for nine innings were ending during the 1946 season.

Controversy always followed Durocher. In July 1946, speaking to a group of reporters in the Polo Grounds, he lamented a recent Dodger trade that had deprived him of his favorite ballplayer, Eddie Stanky, a battler who took on teams with his claws and spikes, as well as his bat. Durocher insisted that even an average player can be a winner if he plays to win, knocking any and all obstacles to success out of the way. Completing his point, Durocher pointed a derisive finger at New York Giants' manager Mel Ott and his men.

"Take a look at them," snorted Durocher. "All nice guys. They'll finish last. Nice guys. Finish last." The next day, Durocher's words were twisted slightly by many reporters, coming out as "Nice guys finish last." The misconstrued remark became probably the most famous quotation in sports and made Durocher the most hated man in New York in the eyes of Giants' fans. Thus, the stage was set for one of the strangest moves in baseball history in July of 1948, when the Dodgers released Durocher and the Giants fired Mel Ott, setting the stage for the manager known in Flatbush as "Mr. Brooklyn" to become the New York manager.

Durocher immediately cleaned house in New York, making it clear he'd be content with a winner and nothing else. He traded away the nucleus of the Giants—including such popular men as slugger Johnny Mize and third baseman Sid Gordon—and picked up scrappy, pugnacious Alvin Dark and Eddie Stanky in trades, as well as menacing Sal Maglie from the doomed Mexican League. Maglie, a pitcher nicknamed "The Barber" for all the close shaves he gave batters (and for his off-season job of cutting hair), won eleven straight games in 1950, helping the Giants achieve a third-place finish in Durocher's second full season. Durocher's team won with his run-and-slash strategy, executing the hit-and-run, sacrifice bunt, and suicide squeeze to win.

In May of 1951, a twenty-year-old rookie outfielder named Willie Mays joined the Giants, and Durocher—always quick to spot authentic talent—coddled him. Brought up to the bigs from Minneapolis of the American Association, where he had been hitting .477, a frightened Mays went 0-for-12, belted a tremendous homer (the first of 660) off the great Warren Spahn, and then went hitless in thirteen more at-bats. Finding his young center fielder in tears, Durocher handled him with understanding and patience, advising the youngster to hike up his uniform to the knees. "You're making the umpires think your strike zone's down where the knees of your pants are," said Durocher, pointing to Mays' pants, which hung down to his ankles. "They're hurting you on the low pitch. Pull up your pants. If you do, you'll get two hits tomorrow."

Mays hiked up his pants, hit a single and triple the next day, and a father-son relationship with Durocher was established. Shortly afterward, Mays tore up National League pitching (twenty homers) en route to Rookie of the Year honors and a Hall-of-Fame career. Mays' emergence as an authentic star highlighted Durocher's 1951 season, his most satisfying as a manager. On August 11, the Giants, which the manager had remade in his own image, trailed the hated first-place Dodgers by thirteen games, but by season's end they had battled "Dem Bums" to a tie (winning the last seven consecutive games).

A three-game playoff ensued, and the teams split the first two games, bringing the deciding contest to the Polo Grounds on October 3. The bottom of the ninth opened with Dodger ace Don Newcombe coasting to a 4–1 win. "Let's win it for Leo," shouted Eddie Stanky, refusing to let the Giants die. Incredibly, the game ended with the Dodgers on the short end of a 5–4 ballgame. The "Miracle at Coogan's Bluff," as it came to be called, was won on Bobby Thomson's tie-breaking homer into the lower deck of the left-field stands. The ball cleared the wall by scant inches, smashing into an empty seat, while radio announcer Russ Hodges screamed five times: "The Giants win the pennant!" The Yankees defeating the Giants in a six-game "subway series" detracted from Durocher's success not a bit. The 1951 Manager of the Year had done the impossible, going from the biggest villain in Polo Grounds' history to its greatest hero.

The Giants faltered for two years with Mays in the army, but in 1954, the "Say-Hey Kid" returned to win the National League's Most Valuable Player award on the strength of a batting title (.345), 41 home runs, and 110 RBIs. Durocher's New Yorkers not only won the pennant over Brooklyn by five games but also overwhelmed Cleveland in the World Series by reeling off four straight wins. Durocher managed like a genius, thanks to pinch hitter

Dusty Rhodes, who singlehandedly won games one (home run), two (single and homer), and three (single) with key hits. "Nothing confounds a pitcher more than having to face a strange batter in a critical situation late in a game," gloated Durocher.[8]

But despite his success, the tactless Durocher made an enemy out of owner Horace Stoneham when the manager's friend, actor Danny Kaye, ridiculed the Giants' executive at a banquet while Leo chortled outrageously. And when New York's pitching staff faltered in 1955, and the team finished third, Stoneham made things difficult for Durocher, who quit to pursue an ill-fated broadcasting career with NBC.

Durocher failed to obtain a managing job for years, settling eventually for a coaching position with the Dodgers in 1961 under his old enemy Walter Alston. Finally, he signed with the hapless Chicago Cubs to manage the 1966 season. For a while Leo the Lip worked his magic, achieving second-place victories in 1969 and 1970 with the long-suffering Cubs, but Durocher seemed incapable of getting along with the better-educated ballplayer of the day, who invariably wore his hair long and questioned authority. "You know what I think of today's ballplayer?" snarled The Lip. "He's a prima donna—spoiled, coddled, lazy."

Durocher left the Cubs in mid-season and a month later joined the struggling Houston franchise to lead the club to a second-place Western Division finish. But once again, the problem was a failure to communicate, and an embittered Durocher quit the game for good in 1973.

Now in his eighties and looking more his age, the still-dapper Durocher rarely emerges from his retreat in Palm Springs, California, except to attend occasional old-timers' games. Overlooked by the Hall of Fame again and again while the less-deserving manager Bucky Harris was selected in 1975, Durocher has lost none of his fire.

"I can manage from my bed better than a lot of guys managing today," snarls Leo. And few would dispute him.

9 ◇ WALT ALSTON: MANAGING YEAR-BY-YEAR

Walter Emmons Alston's entire major-league playing career can be summed up neatly in one paragraph. "Smokey," as his friends have called him ever since the fourth grade because he could throw a ball so fast, played in one major-league game. In 1936, the St. Louis Cardinals called the young first baseman up for a sip—not even a cup—of coffee. Poor and unsophisticated, he spent his short tenure in the majors living in a cheap YMCA room with a bathroom down the hall. He batted against Lonnie Warneke of the Chicago Cubs and failed miserably in his single at-bat. "I fouled off a couple [of pitches], then struck out," Alston liked to say.[1] One of those fouls was a screaming line drive that just missed nicking a foul line for an extra base hit. In the field he had two chances, making one and bobbling the other for an error. "What other major-league manager do you know of who can claim a lifetime batting average of .000 and a lifetime fielding average of .500?" he once said wryly.[2] Shortly thereafter, he was quietly shipped back to the bush leagues and never played another big-league game.

Alston's career might have ended with merely this single citation except for his ability to lead men. When the Dodgers gave him the opportunity to pilot the franchise in November of 1953, he made the most of the opportunity, becoming one of the most successful managers in the history of the game and earning election to the Hall of Fame. In his twenty-three-year managerial career with Brooklyn and Los Angeles, he finished in the second division only three times and won seven pennants. Ironically, however, he never had the job security that lesser managers enjoyed. The Dodger organization always offered him one-year contracts, and he came close to being fired a dozen times. Even the general manager of the Dodgers, Buzzie Bavasi, embarrassed him once by meeting the team on the road in Chicago to deliver a pep talk when the club was on a losing streak. But Alston never considered staging a showdown with officials to demand a long-term contract. "Anything longer would make me nervous," he liked to say.[3] "Signing contracts can mean a lifetime job, if you just keep signing enough of them."

In many ways Walt Alston seemed an unlikely man to command baseball teams in large metropolitan cities such as Brooklyn and—after the club moved following the 1957 season—Los Angeles. He was born on December 1, 1911, in the tiny western Ohio crossroads town of Venice and grew up in Darrtown, a hamlet of 153 persons back in 1954, when he signed his first managerial contract. Emmons, his father, and Lenora, his mother, were sharecroppers until economic conditions forced the elder Alston to take a blue-collar job with the Ford Motor Company. Years later, in the majors, Alston angrily confronted reporters who referred to him in print as a country bumpkin.

In his autobiography, written with Si Burick, *Alston and the Dodgers*, the manager remembered his boyhood with affection. "My Dad . . . worked this land with Mom's help and with the sweat of his brow until I was old enough to assist him with the chores. We had good food to eat and clothes to wear and a pretty good roof over our heads. What we didn't have we bartered for with another tenant or the general store. Next to farming, dad loved baseball best, which accounts for my being a baseball man."[4]

Necks might have been red but hearts were never blue in the Alston household. The family stuck together through lean times. The "pretty good roof over our heads" that Alston later recalled was pretty shabby by contemporary standards. The elder Alston went deep into debt during the twenties but refused to declare bankruptcy because it violated his sense of ethics. He was driven by poverty to move his family by turns into an old shack and later into an abandoned schoolhouse. When things seemed bleakest, the Alstons sought escape through sports, just as millions of Americans in this country have always done. Emmons, Smokey, and two uncles played together on several top flight semipro teams, including the Hamilton Baldwins.

Alston lived at a time when many youngsters were forced to drop out of school to help their families financially, but his parents encouraged him to go to college. The single-most important event of his life may have occurred when a local preacher named Reverend Ralph Jones so believed in Alston's abilities that he paid part of his tuition to send him to school at nearby Miami of Ohio. Not only did the sharecropper's son exhibit the grit and determination needed to graduate in 1935 with a College of Education diploma, but he also starred in baseball and basketball.

As a result, a scout named Frank Rickey—brother of baseball executive Branch Rickey—saw the hard-hitting first baseman in several games and offered him a $135-a-month contract to join the Cardinals' organization. Alston's finest minor-league season was in 1936 with Huntington, West Virginia, of the Mid-Atlantic League. His wrists and forearms were always strong, and later with the Dodgers he used to show off by beating all his players—

including 6'7", 275-pound Frank Howard—in Indian wrestling. He hit a league-leading 35 home runs, drove in 114, and batted .326. The Cardinals brought him up in September, and he flubbed the only opportunity he ever had to play in the big leagues. There was no way he could beat out St. Louis' other star first basemen, Rip Collins and Johnny Mize, and he went down to the minors. Although he could hit a fastball a country acre, he invariably looked foolish with breaking balls and thus languished in the bush leagues until the Cardinals told him that his playing career was over in 1944. Alston was thirty-two, married since his college freshman year to his longtime sweetheart Lela, and proud father of a daughter named Doris. When the Turk—in baseball parlance—came to cut him, the first baseman was shattered, calling it "the nadir of my whole career" in his autobiography.

But four years earlier the Cardinals had made him a playing-manager and his experience kept him in baseball even after his release. Branch Rickey had left the Cards to take a similar job with the Dodgers and offered Alston a player-manager position with Brooklyn's Inter-State League franchise in Trenton, New Jersey. Moving through the system as a minor-league manager, his record was spotty, but he earned two pennants while piloting Montreal of the International League in the early fifties. As a result, when Brooklyn manager Chuck Dressen was released by the organization after the 1953 season (despite winning back-to-back pennants) because of a contract dispute, the Dodgers tapped Alston to command the club. The media called Alston an unknown, but the manager's players didn't feel that way. No less than seventeen members of the team had played under him in the minors.

The boobirds in Ebbets Field screamed for Alston's thinning scalp in 1954, his first season, when he led a team predicted to be a pennant winner to a second-place finish. "I felt the pressure, sure," Alston admitted to writer Donald Honig. "But I don't think I felt it as much as people thought I did. I've always felt that if I did the best I could, I wasn't going to worry about something I couldn't help. I do the best I can and the hell with the rest of it."

But in 1955 the team jelled, finishing thirteen and a half games ahead of the slugging Milwaukee Braves. Brooklyn's roster featured many of the so-called "Boys of Summer" immortalized in author Roger Kahn's fine book by that name, including such electrifying players as Jackie Robinson, Roy Campanella, Pee Wee Reese, Gil Hodges, Don Newcombe, and Duke Snider. Also on that club was a twenty-seven-year-old pitcher with an 0–0 record and a 13.50 ERA named Tom Lasorda who would later bleed Dodger Blue as Alston's unlikely successor.

The highlight of Alston's year came in the seventh game of the World Series when his masterful strategy helped Brooklyn whip the mighty Yankees for the first time.

Offensively, the Dodgers led 1–0 behind the pitching of sturdy Johnny Podres, when Reese led off the sixth inning with a single. Playing for one run, Snider sacrificed Reese to second and was safe himself on an error. Campanella followed up with another sacrifice bunt to put runners on second and third. Gil Hodges stroked a sacrifice fly to bring in the run and the Dodgers led 2–0. The move was typical of the conservative strategy that would characterize Alston as a manager, but he, in return, pointed to his four world championships as evidence that his methods worked.

In the bottom of that same inning, Alston shifted Junior Gilliam from left field to second, replacing him with fleet Sandy Amoros, a left-handed fielder. Yogi Berra strode to the plate with Yankees dancing on first and second with no outs, and Amoros shifted to left-center, where Berra routinely hit some of his most powerful shots. But Podres partially fooled the Yankee catcher, and Berra hit a long opposite field ball that looked destined to land right on the foul line, tying the game. The runners tore around the bases while Amoros raced like a thoroughbred toward the ball, ignored the fence that loomed dangerously near, and speared it on the dead run. What's more, he whirled the ball back to the infield for a double play at first that killed the Yankee rally and ensured a 2–0 series-ending win.

Years later, Alston reminisced about his strategic success. "Could Gilliam have gotten it? You have to wonder. Gilliam wore his glove on his left hand, remember. He would have had to reach across his body to get the ball. Amoros, wearing the glove on his right hand, reaching way out, just did get it."[5]

The following year, Casey Stengel gained sweet revenge on Alston by managing the Yankees to a world championship over Brooklyn, but again the series went to seven games. Sadly, the club's demise came quickly. Robinson retired. Reese was thirty-eight. Campanella, plagued by hand problems and destined to suffer a tragic accident that paralyzed him, was thirty-five—as was strong-armed right fielder Carl Furillo. The Boys of Summer had aged.

Alston set to work rebuilding his tattered team, and he did so through the magnificent Dodger farm system. He also had to deal with declining team morale, caused by the team's move from Brooklyn to Los Angeles for economic reasons after the end of the 1957 season. Only 6,702 fans cheered the team to a third-place finish at the last game played on Ebbets Field turf.

The 1958 season was even worse; Alston weathered a 71–83 seventh-place season, his worst ever as manager. General manager Buzzie Bavasi wanted to offer the job to Alston's predecessor, Chuck Dressen, but Dressen— now Alston's right-hand man as coach—angrily defended the manager, saying "If he goes, I go, too."

But everything went the Dodgers' way in 1959, even though the team's ace was Don Drysdale, with a lackluster 17–13 season. Alston's men played in a makeshift stadium until a new home could be built, but the distraction didn't halt the team's success.

Power hitters Wally Moon and Duke Snider overcame the stadium's deficiencies to hit nineteen and twenty-three home runs, respectively. Thirty-five-year-old Gil Hodges clubbed twenty-five home runs. A fleet rookie named Maury Wills joined the team, and even the aging Snider contributed a .308 performance as the Dodgers beat the Braves in a two-game playoff for another pennant. Moreover, in only its second year of existence, Los Angeles gained a world championship by defeating the Chicago White Sox in a six-game series.

Alston was wise enough to see that the makeup of his club had changed, and he altered his strategy accordingly. Traditionally the Dodgers had been a power hitting club. Now he relied on speed, defense, and Sandy Koufax's wonderful arm to make Los Angeles jell.

But in spite of having accumulated an enviable record, Alston never could make all of his players happy. "Walter knew baseball as well as anyone, but he was slow-witted," Johnny Roseboro once charged. "He missed some opportunities because he didn't see them soon enough and seize them fast enough. There were certain choices that the manager was supposed to make for us, but sometimes we'd look over at Walter and he'd shrug as if to say, 'I dunno, do what you think best.' " Roseboro concluded with a lefthanded compliment: "Because he was conservative, Walter made fewer mistakes than any other manager I ever saw."[6]

Roseboro was correct in his assessment. Alston consistently won despite adhering to the most close-to-the-vest strategy of his era. A Leo Durocher or Fred Haney of the Braves might gamble in late innings to throw opposing managers off balance, but the country boy from Darrtown always went by the book.

What the players failed to realize was that Alston always hired sound baseball men as coaches—such as Leo

Durocher, Chuck Dressen, and Jim Gilliam—who were as liberal as he was conservative. The manager not only consulted these men regularly, he gave them authority to act when necessary, and he always backed them up. In business one of the signs of a good leader is the ability to select quality personnel. And Alston didn't choose men who merely carried out his orders; he wanted people who were aggressive to complement his own personality.

When Wills broke in as a fleet rookie in 1959, it irritated Dodgers such as Roseboro when Alston ordered batters to lay down sacrifice bunts to get the speedy Wills down to second instead of letting him steal the bag. But by 1962, when Wills had gained enough baseball savvy to know the moves of most opposing big-league pitchers, he had the green light to steal from his manager. As a result, Wills went from 35 stolen bases in 1961 to 104 thefts in 1962, shattering a major-league record set by Ty Cobb back in 1915. "The fact that he relied on my judgment inspired me with confidence," admitted Wills. "The thing that pleased me most was that I was able to come through for him every time. . . . As long as he was going to rely on my opinion the least I could do was to make him look good.

"I know that as far as handling men, no one is better at it than Walt Alston. He doesn't crack a whip or needle us. He treats us like men, and expects us to act that way. Sometimes we act like boys, but at least he gives us credit for being mature. He doesn't watch over us, and few Dodgers ever have taken advantage of him."[7]

Alston himself seemed immune to his players' criticism, although it surely hurt him. He received the brunt of his criticism from players who were being platooned. Except for Wills and outstanding pitchers such as Koufax and reliever Mike Marshall, Los Angeles had ceased to be a team of stars. Hodges went to the Mets in 1962, and soon-forgotten men such as Daryl Spencer, Lee Walls, Larry Burright, and Tim Harkness wore Dodger Blue.

Incredibly, the manager led them to victory over victory, and the season came down to a playoff with the hated Giants, which San Francisco won in three games. Alston went by the book, playing his best left-handed batters against righty pitchers and vice versa. "I don't get too many comments from my players about strategy," said Alston. "They're content to let you do the worrying."[8] Like Earl Weaver and Casey Stengel, platooning worked well for him, but it bothered team malcontents.

"Generally, you don't have to worry about the guys who are playing every day," shrugged Alston. "It's the guys who are sitting on the bench that are the ones that get needles in their pants. . . . I think anyone who's a good athlete and a good competitor has to be a little high-strung; it's part of what makes them what they are. You've got to understand it. . . . In the past few years I've had guys on the bench who were just about as good as the guys playing."[9]

But few men found fault with the quiet Dodger manager as a person. "Alston was a man of integrity," said Roseboro. "He didn't have much to say, but he meant what he did say. He didn't lie or try to con us. He was a clean, decent man, on and off the field. He knew ballplayers aren't saints and knew we were doing some things off the field we shouldn't, but the line he drew was where the team morale would be disrupted. He treated the team as if it were his family. He was the sort of father who didn't interfere in everything his boys did but would disown anyone who was disrespectful."[10]

Steve Garvey, in his autobiography *Garvey*, agreed with that assessment. "Walter Alston taught me patience and a professional attitude about baseball," said Garvey, L.A.'s slugging star of the seventies. "He also taught me about respect."[11]

Alston led his team to world championships in 1963 and 1965, then won the pennant in 1966. The hero of the 1963 season was Koufax, who went 25–5, struck out 311 batters, and enjoyed a 1.88 earned run average. Koufax also proved a hero in 1965 when he enjoyed a 27–9 mark and pitched two shutouts in the World Series.

The manager won his last pennant in 1974, winning on a strategy of pitching iron-armed Mike Marshall whenever a game was on the line. Marshall appeared in a record 106 games, and the Dodgers now had a solid infield with Garvey at first, Davey Lopes at second, Bill Russell at short, and Ron Cey at third. But the strain of managing began to show on Alston, and after disappointing second-place finishes in 1975 and 1976, he decided against asking for one more renewable contract.

In 1976, the same year that Braves slugger Hank Aaron called it quits after belting 755 career home runs, Walt Alston retired to his Ohio farm after twenty-three consecutive years of managing the Dodgers. Only the fabled John McGraw and Connie Mack enjoyed longer reigns with a single club, and in 1983, he joined these two gentlemen in the Hall of Fame. The following year, he died of a heart attack, but he left behind these words of wisdom.

"The most important part of managing? Be your own self. To me that's probably the most important part of it, more so than the strategy part. If you know yourself, you'll know your players—how to handle them, how to keep them happy, how to get a hundred percent out of them, which ones to pat on the back, which ones to give a kick in the ass now and then. I occasionally raise hell at meetings if I think it's for the good of the whole club, but mostly I take a guy into the office and talk to him. The winning of the ball game and the good of the team come first."[12]

◇ 10 ◇ EARL WEAVER: LORD BALTIMORE

A timeworn baseball adage insists that a manager doesn't have much influence on his club. He cannot help a bad team, and he can only injure a good team.

Earl Weaver, the former Baltimore manager who achieved five 100-win seasons during his fifteen-and-a-half seasons in the major leagues, has always disagreed with that saying. "A good manager can help a bad team win a few more games, and he can make a good team win a championship," he claimed.[1]

The man known to millions by such nicknames as "Lord Baltimore," the "Earl of Baltimore," and the "Bismarck of Baltimore," never played an inning in the major leagues, but his Orioles only finished once out of the first division during his career. His teams, in fact, came in first or second thirteen times. "Bad ballplayers make good managers," he has frequently declared. His Orioles won one world championship (1970), four pennants (1969, 1970, 1971, 1979) and six American League East championships (1969, 1970, 1971, 1973, 1974, 1979). No wonder that former Cleveland Indians president Gabe Paul said,

"I don't know if Earl Weaver is the greatest manager of all time, but he is close."[2]

When Earl Sidney Weaver was born in St. Louis on August 14, 1930, his parents envisioned a career for him in baseball. Clothing dry cleaner Earl M. Weaver and his wife Ethel bought their son Earl a baseball uniform when he was only five. The boy wore it daily while his father and grandfather took turns pitching to him in the backyard. Being a major leaguer might seem an abstract goal too lofty to consider for most boys, but not for Earl. After all, his father cleaned the uniforms of both the hometown Browns and Cardinals and frequently brought his son into the locker rooms of both teams when he went upon his appointed rounds.

The main strike that young Weaver had against him as a young player was his small stature. (With the Orioles, he later endured many barbs because of his height, including this rip by pitcher Jim Palmer: "Did you ever notice how Earl always goes to the highest spot on the mound when he comes out?") But his hustle and inward fire impressed high school coach Ray Elliot at St. Louis' Beaumont High School so much that Weaver made the team as a freshman in 1944. That 1944 Beaumont team was one of the most talented high school teams ever assembled, listing future major leaguers Roy Sievers, Bobby Hofman, Bobby Weisler, and Jimmy Goodwin on the roster, as well as the scrappy Weaver.

Elliot was the first coach to teach Weaver the importance of fundamentals, even working his players indoors in a gym all winter. "Back then, that was revolutionary," Weaver told *Baltimore Evening Sun* sportswriter Terry Pluto. "Some people thought he was crazy with all the [indoor] drills he put us through. . . . He was ahead of his time and he was part of the reason we won city titles."

But while Weaver was an exceptional ballplayer, attracting attention from major-league scouts before he was fourteen, he proved to be only a so-so student despite his raw intelligence. Years later, as a major-league manager and professional broadcaster, he became famous for his assaults upon the English language—particularly, in Weaver parlance, "when I went banana cake." But the boy was practically a Rhodes scholar when it came to studying and understanding baseball.

"Between the Cardinals and old Browns, I went to a hundred games a summer," recalled Weaver. "I used to watch the games closely. I would be there, mulling over and second guessing the moves of [Cardinals' manager] Billy Southworth. Hell, I was twelve years old and I thought I knew more than he did."[3]

The seventeen-year-old Weaver received a modest contract with the St. Louis Cardinals after graduation, accepting a signing bonus of $1,500 and a monthly salary of $175. He attended his first minor-league spring training camp and thought he had earned a roster spot with Duluth in Class C ball. However, the Cardinal brass disagreed and ordered him to report to their Class D West Frankfort, Illinois, franchise. The demotion proved to be a disguised blessing. "Two months later the Duluth team bus crashed and ten of those kids were killed," revealed Weaver in his autobiography, *It's What You Learn After You Know It All That Counts* (1983). He believed that not only his career, but his life, might have ended had he boarded that bus.

Weaver's professional career began dramatically. The 5'6", 155-pound second baseman belted a home run his first time at bat and finished the season as the team's MVP for the pennant-winning West Frankfort club. But lonely in the bush-league town, the youngster married a girl from St. Louis named Jane Johnston. The match was unhappy, partially because Weaver's obsession with baseball kept him away from home so often, and ended in divorce in 1963. The couple had three children.

That first minor-league home run, unfortunately, was

not indicative of many more to come. Cursed with less than major-league hitting skills, Weaver struggled in the minors, attending only one big-league spring training camp. Like other mediocre players he studied the game and developed his own theories of baseball strategy. He became a playing-manager for the independently owned Knoxville Smokies in 1956. The following year, he began managing in Fitzgerald, Georgia, for the Baltimore Orioles farm system, putting his aspirations to play second base in the majors behind him. He retired with a career .267 average to show for thirteen seasons in the minors and a new wife—Marianna—who he met while managing in Elmira.

As a manager, Weaver immediately impressed Harry Dalton, then the Orioles director of player personnel, with his ability to handle young players. Dalton promoted the fiery skipper year-by-year. "It dawned on me that he would make a helluva major-league manager," said Dalton.[4]

In 1966 and 1967, Weaver led the Triple A Rochester Red Wings to first- and second-place finishes respectively. In 1968, Weaver finally achieved his dream of making the major leagues when the Orioles hired him as a first-base coach. And when manager Hank Bauer's Orioles faltered midway through the 1968 season, with the team fourteen games out of first place, the swaggering, greying Weaver became the new Bird pilot.

Sportswriters and rival managers alike quickly recognized Weaver's genius. After taking over the team from Bauer, Weaver guided the club to a 48–34 third-place finish. The manager proved immediately that he was a master field boss. He had original ideas about how the game should be played, and a legion of managers soon imitated his philosophies. Weaver pooh-poohed the notion that major-league players, being grown men, needed to have their confidence built up. "Lesson Number One is psychology don't mean anything in baseball and I don't want to hear you ask me about momentum," he snarled at Terry Pluto. "Ain't no such thing."

What Weaver *did* believe in was the necessity of knowing his ballplayers' strengths and weaknesses. For that reason, like New York Yankee manager Casey Stengel, he platooned his ballplayers to get the most out of the talents of all twenty-five men on his roster. "The key to managing is player evaluation," said Weaver, "which is another way of saying that you must know which buttons to push and when to push them."[5]

Weaver found the right buttons to press on the 1969 Orioles, developing them into one of the game's greatest teams. During the 1969 spring training he drilled his players on fundamentals and stressed the importance of playing for big innings. He scorned the practice of relying upon sacrifice bunts to score only a single run in an inning, believing that such "automatic outs" were detrimental to his club and only worked back in the so-called "dead ball" era. "I'd like to find the guy who invented the sacrifice bunt and shove it in his ear," Weaver told sportswriter Thomas Boswell of *The Washington Post.* "In the early and middle innings, it's the most overused strategy in baseball. Play for one run early and lose by one run late."

Weaver became famous for advocating three-run homers as the best offensive weapon to win games, and there was no doubt he had the personnel to deliver. The 1969 Orioles belted 175 home runs, led by Boog Powell (37), Brooks Robinson (23), Frank Robinson (32), and Paul Blair (26). The Orioles' pitching staff was no less spectacular, bolstered by such stars as Mike Cuellar (23–11), Dave McNally (20–7), sore-backed Jim Palmer (16–4), and twenty-four-year-old Tom Phoebus (14–7). Unlike Bauer, his predecessor, who believed in using a five-man pitching rotation, Weaver preferred to go with four starters. "A four-man rotation . . . gives the pitchers chances for more wins," said Weaver. "It means more starts for each pitcher. I look at it this way: if you have four pitchers who are winning for you, and you can get them to the mound more often, it means more wins for the team. The starts you give to your fifth-best starter are taken away from the four who are better than him."[6]

Unfortunately, after winning the division nineteen games ahead of second-place Detroit with a 109–53 record, the Orioles came unglued against New York's National Leaguers in the 1969 World Series. The so-called Miracle Mets lost the first game to Mike Cuellar, then stunned the heavily favored Birds in the next four games to become world champions. Losing to the Mets devastated Weaver. "The loss didn't sit well on my stomach," he later recalled. "When I got home I threw up."[7] After that humbling experience, he began to often repeat his favorite saying, "It's what you learn after you know it all that counts."

But Weaver and his Orioles rebounded from their embarrassing World Series loss. The manager became known as one of the hardest-working men in the game. He became fanatically interested in statistics, keeping up-to-date files on how American League batters and pitchers fared against Baltimore pitchers and batters. "I use my statistics to decide on changing pitchers," said Weaver in his book, *Weaver on Strategy* (1984). "Let's say it's a crucial game, and Jim Palmer is pitching to Graig Nettles. Nettles is a .375 hitter against Palmer, but my stats show that he's only two for twenty-two against Tippy, so I'll bring in Martinez to face Nettles. The decision is made for you."

Like Connie Mack, who insisted on using a lucky pencil, the Oriole manager always used his lucky pen to condense his stats and put them on index cards the day of a game. He also read through extensive computerized reports prepared by his scouts, but he insisted on interpreting the information himself.

Another tactic of Weaver's was umpire-baiting, a habit that caused the men-in-blue to throw him out of nearly a hundred games during his career. He was even ejected from a World Series game in 1969, the first manager in thirty-four years to suffer such a fate.

Curiously, these supposedly impartial umpires often publicly announced their aversion to Weaver. "I hate Earl Weaver with a passion," said Ron Luciano, the umpire-turned-broadcaster. "I met him in my second year of base-ball. I threw him out that first night and three nights after that." Umpire Nick Bremigan likened him to Iran's Aya-tollah, and Jim Evans, another arbiter, compared him to the Son of Sam, a New York mass murderer. "He never shuts up," complained Marty Springstead. "The way to test a Timex watch would be to strap it to Weaver's tongue."

Weaver's misadventures with umpires became part of baseball legend. In the minors he protested what he thought was a blown call at third base by literally stealing third base and carting it into the clubhouse, delaying the game for more than ten minutes until a groundskeeper could talk him into giving it back. In the major leagues Weaver once tore a rulebook to shreds after he thought an umpire missed an interference call by a Cleveland catcher on a Baltimore bunt. He's been suspended for bumping umpires and kicking dirt between their legs. He's embarrassed umpires by pretending to kick *them* out of games for blowing calls. On one occasion, umpire Rick Garcia threw Weaver out of a game, only to later find the manager hiding in the dugout bathroom.

In his defense, Weaver argued that he harangued um-pires to keep them honest. Indeed, many of his fellow managers believed Weaver received more than his share of close calls because umpires feared his wrath. And the Baltimore manager argued with justification that he knew the rulebook as well or better than they did. In 1977, he charged out onto the field after Cleveland had scored two runs on an overthrow by Rich Dauer at second to appar-ently win the game 4–3 when Tribe runner Jim Norris raced from first to home. Both teams exited into the clubhouse while an irate Weaver read umpire Marty Springstead rule 7:05 (g), stating that a runner gets only two bases on an overthrow. "Earl is 150 percent right," ruled Marty Springstead. "We've got to continue the game and Norris goes back to third base."[8] One inning later, Baltimore scored twice to snatch a 5–3 win away from the stunned Indians.

Without question, Weaver was the dominant manager of the seventies, with six American League championships to his credit. His 1970 and 1971 Orioles won 108 and 101 games respectively en route to American League pennants. Weaver's Birds won the World Series in 1970 against Cincinnati but the following year lost to Pittsburgh in seven games. His failure to win more series championships irritated him, and he endured the taunts of umpires such as Bill Haller, who invariably brought up this deficiency during on-the-diamond arguments.

As a strategist, however, Weaver had no deficiencies, always staying three or four innings ahead of the present game situation so that he was seldom surprised by another manager's late-inning moves. Unlike Cincinnati manager Pete Rose, who has faced several mutinies from unhappy members of his bullpen because he has them up-and-throwing too many times in a game, Weaver only warmed up his relief pitchers when he intended to use them. As a result, Baltimore's starting pitchers felt less tension on the mound and consequently performed better. "Earl has great confidence in his starters and the pitchers feel the same way toward him," former big-league manager George Bamberger told Terry Pluto. "That's why [Oriole pitchers] don't look over their shoulders to the dugout or bullpen when they get into a jam."

Nonetheless, Weaver admitted that he looked for certain tell-tale signs that warned him his starters were about to falter. When hitters began to send screaming fouls past the first and third base coaching boxes instead of fouling them straight back, the manager knew that opposing batters were timing his pitcher—particularly if the number seven and eight men in the lineup were beginning to connect. A mental bell also went off in Weaver's head if his pitcher walked a leadoff batter, thereby putting himself in hot water. The manager had great confidence in his catcher and could tell by a backstop's mannerisms if a pitcher had suddenly lost his stuff.[9]

Weaver was also a master at creating a twenty-five-man roster. Where Cincinnati's Rose endures dissension because he's overstocked with stars who complain when they don't play regularly, Weaver often won with players that other clubs had cast off. By knowing their strengths in given situations, the manager squeezed the best out of their abilities, thus making household names out of part-time performers such as John Lowenstein who hit .320, belted 24 homers, and knocked in 66 runs in a scant 322 at-bats in 1982. "The man's a genius at finding situations where an average player—like me—can look like a star because a lot of subtle factors are working in [my] favor," said Lowenstein. "He has a passion for finding the perfect player for the perfect spot."[10]

Weaver preached adherence to certain absolutes that his players seldom violated. With a left-handed pull hitter at the plate and a man on first, the manager rarely ordered a steal. "Take advantage of the hole you get when the first baseman plays close to the bag," Weaver commanded his runners. The manager, incidentally, kept track of the success rate of his runners. "For the steal to be worthwhile, the runner should be safe about 75 percent of the time," said Weaver. "The player who steals thirty-five bases but is thrown out twenty-five times isn't helping the team. If I had a runner stealing thirty-five bases out of sixty attempts, I'd stop giving him the steal sign."[11]

But in 1982, at the relatively young age of fifty-two, Weaver sensed that his fiery spirit had dimmed some and he retired, leaving the game with enviable win-loss totals of 1,354–919, his .596 percentage the third-best in major-league history. His 1982 season disappointed him. The season came down to a 10–2 loss to Milwaukee in Weaver's final game, giving the Brewers the pennant by one game over Baltimore.

In 1985, the manager made the mistake of accepting an annual $500,000 contract to again manage his beloved Birds, replacing the fired Joe Altobelli. He managed to bring the team in fourth in 1985, but in 1986 the Birds finished dead last. For the first time in his career, a Weaver team played below .500 ball. Not even Weaver's frantic shuffling of 141 different lineups could stop the Baltimore slide into mediocrity.

Nonetheless, Weaver's accomplishments as a manager certainly override the sad conclusion to his career. As sportswriter Tom Boswell once said about the Earl of Baltimore, "Weaver is the bloom of native American wit and savvy as revealed within our national pastime."[12] The manager almost certainly will qualify for a spot in the Hall of Fame as soon as he is eligible in 1992.

11 ◇ SPARKY ANDERSON: FROM CAR SALESMAN TO LEGEND

While many great managers establish their reputations with a single team, Sparky Anderson has demonstrated his winning ways with two clubs, the Cincinnati Reds and the Detroit Tigers. He holds the rare distinction of being the first manager to win world championships with clubs in the National *and* the American Leagues, as well as the first to win a hundred games or more in both leagues.

But even as a minor-league player, Anderson reasoned like a manager. Back in 1954, the weak-hitting Anderson had one of his finest years, batting .296 with Pueblo, Colorado, of the Class A Western League and was promoted the next spring to Fort Worth of the Texas League. Nervous and overanxious to please his manager, Tommy Holmes, Anderson had a horrendous spring, but still Fort Worth retained him. In his 1978 autobiography, *The Main Spark*, Anderson says that Holmes' example was the first valuable lesson that later helped him in his own managerial career: "Don't be too rough in your judgment of a player who isn't doing well in spring training."

Like Tommy Lasorda and Walter Alston, Anderson

never achieved greatness as a player. This house painter's son of Norwegian ancestry was born in the unlikeliest state to produce a baseball hero—South Dakota—on February 22, 1934, but fortunately, his family moved to Los Angeles looking for better job opportunities with World War Two plants when he was eight. California friends called him "Sparky" because he always played with enthusiasm and fearlessness; years later, in the minor leagues, he often wiped out catchers at home plate who were twice his size with *kamikaze* slides. Sparky's problem as a youngster was that he didn't know where to draw the line no matter what sport he played. In a 1974 interview with *Sports Illustrated*, Anderson sheepishly recalled how he knocked an opponent in a basketball game through two glass doors. "I thought I'd killed him," he said. "I used to be crazy."

Anderson was a poor boy who lived with eight other relatives in a two-bedroom house located in a seedy L.A. neighborhood near the University of Southern California. His Uncle Elmer had played Class D ball, and Sparky's father was always ready to play a game of catch with him. But it was the Anderson family's proximity to the college that fostered the youngster's dream of becoming a professional player. The coach of the famed USC Trojans was Rod Dedeaux, a legend in college circles. One day Anderson returned a lost baseball to Dedeaux, and the amused coach invited him to be his batboy. To Dedeaux's surprise, the youngster stayed in the job five years, gleaning every ounce of baseball knowledge he could take from the master, but turned down an offer from the coach to attend college himself on a baseball scholarship. To this day no one has ever accused Anderson of being a college graduate. His abuses of grammar are second in legend only to Casey Stengel.

Instead, at nineteen, Anderson signed a $250-a-month contract to play Class C ball in the Dodger organization, hoping his hard-nosed style of play would offset his physical limitations. Unfortunately, they didn't. Umpires ejected him from sixteen games his freshman year with Santa Barbara of the California League for various forms of unsportsmanlike conduct, and he had to learn to curtail his fiery attitude.

The scrappy Anderson never had an opportunity to break in with the talent-rich Dodgers, but he did get an opportunity to play major-league ball in the 1959 season after the Phillies obtained him in a trade. Philadelphia gave him a season-long opportunity to make the club, but he batted only .218 in 152 games for the last-place team. Afterwards, the franchise demoted him to Toronto, then a Triple A club, where he gained fame as a "good field–no hit" second baseman. At Toronto in 1960, his manager was Chuck Dressen, who had won back-to-back pennants with Brooklyn before making the fatal mistake of demanding a three-year contract from Dodger management.

Dressen recognized the innate potential that Anderson had for managing, and he taught the prematurely white-haired second baseman all the little tricks he himself had learned while a pilot in the big leagues since 1934. Dressen emphasized the need to force the opposing manager to "exhaust his bench strength" and to know precisely when a pitcher had lost his stuff on the mound. "I have a feeling for pitchers and I learned it from Charlie," Anderson once said. "He knew more about pitchers than anybody I've ever been around."[1]

Anderson worked an apprenticeship as a minor-league manager during the sixties and supported his family by working as a used car salesman in the off-season for seven years. His years of struggle were rewarded in 1969 when the expansion-era San Diego Padres signed him as a coach. Once back in the big leagues, success came overnight. The Cincinnati Reds hired him as manager in 1970, and he moved his wife Carol [his bride back when both were nineteen] and family to Ohio, never dreaming that he was about to become the National League Manager of the Year. The thirty-five-year-old Anderson was to become the most successful manager in Cincinnati's century-old history, winning two world championships, four pennants, and five division titles.

The Reds under Sparky Anderson became known as "The Big Red Machine," a club whose power frequently was compared with the 1927 and 1961 Yankees. Anderson inherited an essentially healthy club from deposed manager Dave Bristol. The 1969 Reds, led by Pete Rose's second straight National League batting championship, came up short against Atlanta for the Western Division title despite a whopping team batting average of .276.

Fans and writers alike deplored Cincinnati general manager Bob Howsam's choice of "that busher" for manager. But Howsam had known Anderson during the latter's minor-league managing days and considered him not only a brilliant strategist but also a straight-shooting leader who knew how to command respect. "At no time have I ever thought about hiring a manager to get favorable public reaction," Howsam snapped at his critics. "I hired Anderson because I felt he was the best man available to do the job we wanted done by our standards."

The 5'10", 170-pound Anderson liked the team he inherited from Bristol. That 1970 squad included twenty-two-year-old Dave Concepcion; slugging Tony Perez; hustling team captain Pete Rose, whose style of play out-Andersoned even Sparky Anderson; future Hall-of-Famer Johnny Bench; and a hitting star in the making named Hal McRae. That first year the Reds won 102 games, finishing fourteen-and-a-half games ahead of Los Angeles in the Western Division. And in the playoffs, the Reds swept three games from Roberto Clemente and the Pirates, earning the opportunity to face Earl Weaver's Orioles in the World Series. Even though Baltimore upset Anderson's charges in a five-game series, Anderson felt no shame over what he had accomplished his freshman season. Johnny Bench, only twenty-two, won the Most Valuable Player award by socking 45 home runs, collecting

148 runs batted in, and hitting .293. Tony Perez and Lee May celebrated the Reds' move into new Riverfront Stadium by collectively hitting 74 homers, while Pete Rose led the league with 205 hits. "Those Cincinnati years were just a manager's dream," Anderson later said. "How often do you get a Johnny Bench, a Pete Rose, a Joe Morgan, a Tony Perez—a Hall of Fame dream team at its peak that you sort of inherit your first year as a major-league manager? I was real lucky."[2]

Anderson suffered a sophomore jinx in 1971, when his injury-riddled club limped to a disappointing fourth-place finish but came back in 1972 to win the division, losing to Oakland in the playoffs. The 1973 season was an instant replay of the previous year. Anderson's Red Machine again won the division, but this time the Mets beat them in the playoffs.

Without question the manager's greatest year occurred in 1975. That Cincinnati club not only rolled to an easy division title with 108 wins, but it also won three-of-three from the Pirates in the playoffs to win the right to meet Boston in the World Series.

Anderson's greatest bit of strategy in 1975 came in May, when the Reds were playing 12–12 ball and looking anything like a championship club. The manager approached Pete Rose, who had spent the entire 1974 season in the outfield. "I'd like you to try third base."

"When?" asked Rose.

"Tomorrow," said Anderson, and the next night Charlie Hustle inherited the unfamiliar position from banjo-hitting John Vukovich.[3] Rose's move to third allowed twenty-two-year-old George Foster to crack the outfield lineup, and the youngster responded with 23 home runs and 78 runs batted in. Curiously, the shift to third only seemed to help Rose's game. He batted .317, second on the club to second baseman Joe Morgan's .327. Morgan also hit 17 home runs, drove in 94 runs, and stole 67 bases to become the National League's Most Valuable Player.

Anderson took a hungry club into the World Series against Boston. The Reds sought their first world title in thirty-five years and won it in a classic seven-game series that wasn't decided until the ninth inning of the final contest on a single by Joe Morgan for a 4–3 win. The next year seemed anticlimactic as the Red Machine again bowled over National League competition and trimmed the mighty New York Yankees easily in four straight series wins.

Following the sweep of the Yankees, the first successful defense of a world championship by a National League team in fifty years, Anderson was characteristically modest. "Don't make managing out to be a lot more than it is," he said. "The only people who win games are the ones out there on the field." Pete Rose disagreed, giving credit for the spectacular season to Anderson, saying, "We'd walk through hell in a gasoline suit for him."[4]

Joe Morgan, a thoughtful man, once explained what made Anderson a winner. "Ninety percent of managing is psychology, and how you keep players prepared to play," he told reporter Michael Rozek. "When I played for Sparky, the attitude he had with us was the reason why we won all those championships. I really didn't think of him as my manager, but more like he was part of my family—and I'll do a lot more for my family than I will my manager."

Anderson believes in managing from the dugout, not from the clubhouse. As a result, he seldom calls team meetings. "The more you stand up there, the better chance they have of finding out how dumb you are," he told *Sports Illustrated*.

But after finishing second in 1977 and again in 1978, the club paid Anderson not to manage in 1979. Anderson's firing by Cincinnati was unexpected. He met with Cincinnati general manager Dick Wagner one day over breakfast to talk about the reorganization of the team and received his pink slip along with his order of eggs. "After I was fired, it put a fire in my belly that burned until I proved 'em wrong," said Anderson in an interview published after he'd won a world championship with Detroit. "Ever since the day they fired me, I wanted to prove 'em wrong, and I did, finally. It took a while, but I did it."[5]

Anderson spent a year as a broadcaster, mangling the English language as Dizzy Dean had once done. But in 1980, he was back in baseball, taking over the Detroit Tigers, a perennial American League second-division team. Slowly but surely, the manager cut all deadwood. Eight years after he arrived in Tigertown, only three players of his original twenty-five-man roster remained with the club, and in fact, only five remained in the game—period.

With the Tigers, Anderson inherited a team that had a history of losing ways, but he liked what he saw in the farm system. The manager said that he prefers building a club by bringing up youngsters from the minor leagues to trying to buy pennants with free agents the way that California's Gene Autry and New York's George Steinbrenner have tried to do. "See, I'm a little different," Anderson has said. "Most managers think winning creates chemistry. I think chemistry creates winning—that the way the guys you have work together makes you, as a manager, a winner."[6]

Anderson didn't take long to turn the franchise around. "He came and changed the team," Lou Whitaker told reporter Vern Plagenhoef. "I'm not saying we had no class, but we didn't have clothes. We went from no-dress to best-dressed." In 1984 the club won ten of its first eleven games and thirty-five of its first forty en route to winning the American League East by fifteen games. A stalwart Kansas City team was shredded in three straight playoff games, and the San Diego Padres were dispatched with equal ease in five games.

In Detroit, Anderson began a tradition he had begun in Cincinnati of yanking starting pitchers the minute his instincts told him they were going bad. Back in 1976, for example, Reds' reliever Rawly Eastwick led the league with twenty-six saves and turned in a sparkling eleven wins to boot. Anderson has managed in twenty-eight World Series games for the Tigers and Reds, but only one pitcher (Detroit's Jack Morris) has ever thrown a complete game. No wonder sportswriters have dubbed the manager "Captain Hook."

But during the 1984 season, newly acquired reliever Willie Hernandez teamed up with Señor Smoke, portly Aurelio Lopez, to give the Tigers a relief crew that put out more fires than Red Adair. Hernandez appeared in a league-leading eighty games and contributed thirty-two saves to give him both MVP and Cy Young honors in the American League.

Anderson also wins because he has always been a master at delegating authority, whether it be to his coaches or his players. After winning the World Series with Detroit, the manager revealed in a magazine interview that he seldom called pitches from the dugout. "Once in a while [I will], when we have a particular strategy in mind," shrugged Anderson, "but we have such a great catcher in Lance Parrish now that we don't do it very much. I trust his judgment."[7]

In 1987, Anderson took a poorly rated club that had no regular catcher at the beginning of the season and platooned his way into the American League playoffs. And although he lost to Minnesota, he was named the American League's Manager of the Year in honor of his mastery.

Despite his success, Anderson's critics accuse him of managing more with his heart than with his head, saying that too many of his decisions are based on gut impulses. His supporters call the charge nonsense, believing that the manager doesn't need to consult computer cards a la Earl Weaver to make decisions; Anderson stores statistics in his head. He's also a stickler for fundamentals and the need to play heads-up baseball. "Don't miss a sign unless you're legally blind" is his motto.

Curiously, Anderson still wins even though he's mellowed over the years. The Reds of 1970 would hardly recognize the laid-back boss of the 1988 Tigers. He still wants to win as much as ever, but he doesn't knock people through glass windows any longer to gain a victory. Nor does he believe a manager need drink his sorrows away after losing a close one.

"I never could understand the managers who needed a few shooters [shots] after they lost," Anderson told *The Detroit News'* Tom Gage in the final weeks of the 1987 season. "What good does that do? They then wake up with real problems, because that's when their head is pounding.

"I still care about winning, but I don't take losing as hard as I once did. I have dinner plans Saturday night [after an important game with Toronto], win or lose."

Win or lose, Anderson is now used to the fickle ways of baseball fans. As a manager, his is not to reason why, his is just to bear the fans' outcry. "As the manager, you represent to the fans the essence of the team. If you win, they love you, and if you lose, it ain't a question of they *hate* you—they don't even *know* you—but you represent what they don't like: a loser. . . . That's the way they are. And it's part of the job."

12 WHITEY HERZOG: THE MAN WHO PAID HIS DUES

Whitey Herzog may have been the manager of the best team in the National League in 1987, but he hasn't come all that far. The reason for that seemingly contradictory statement is that he was born in New Athens, Illinois, a country town of 1,400 farmers and coal miners of German ancestry, just 40 miles from St. Louis. Herzog often claims that his New Athens upbringing has never left him; he was taught to be prompt and tidy, and he values people who are on time and well organized. Woe to the ballplayer who shows up a few minutes before game time or whose locker smells as if something died in it that week.

Born on November 9, 1931, Herzog came from blue-collar stock. Neither Edgar, his father, nor Lietta, his mother, ever graduated from high school, and as a youth he worked as a gravedigger, among other things, to help out his parents. His full name was Dorrel Norman Elvert Herzog; thus, he was suitably grateful when a minor-league manager, Johnny Pesky, called him the "White Rat," a nickname that soon was shortened to "Whitey," plain and simple. "Anything is better than Dorrel, I suppose," he maintains.[1]

Herzog was never much of a student, but he saw to it that his grades stayed just high enough to maintain his eligibility for high school sports. There wasn't much for him to do in New Athens but work, date Mary Lou Sinn—his wife since 1953—and play ball, so he did as much of the latter two activities as his parents would allow.

"There was always somebody to play ball with. I'd have never made the big leagues, never become a big-league manager, never made the kind of money I've made, if I hadn't been a small-town kid with nothing to do but play ball," he wrote in his 1987 autobiography (co-written with Kevin Horrigan), *White Rat*. "Kids today don't realize the way it was back then. It was nothing for us to play five or six nine-inning games every day. We'd play uptown against downtown, choose up sides with a bat. . . . We'd get more at-bats in one day than kids today get in a whole season of Little League."

By the time he reached high school, Herzog became a confirmed baseball addict, skipping his classes to watch the Browns and Cardinals play at Sportsman's Park. He always sneaked past a stadium chain to get into the upper deck to grab batting practice fouls before a game. "I'd take the balls back downstairs when the game started and sell four of them for a buck apiece, and still go home with a couple. . . . I'd have enough profits for a couple of hot dogs and a Coke, and I'd go home with two brand new baseballs."[2]

Despite his poor grades and relative small size (5'10", 150 pounds), young Herzog was a good enough basketball and baseball player to be offered seven college scholarships. However, he believed that his future was in baseball, not academics, and he signed a $1,500 bonus contract with the New York Yankees—more, he likes to brag, than Mickey Mantle was paid.

To make a long story short, Herzog's minor-league career began in 1949 with the McAlester (OK) Rockets in the Class D Sooner State League. He knocked around the bushes for seven years before getting an opportunity to play with the lowly Washington Senators in 1956. At that time an old saying referring to the Senators from the 1920s was revived. Players said that "Washington was first in war, first in peace, and last in the American League."

The twenty-five-year-old Herzog played but thirty-six games in 1957 for the last-place Senators, batting an abysmal .167. He was sent to the minors in 1958. The Senators decided they were too good for the likes of him and sent the youngster to the Kansas City team, which then consistently finished in seventh place, one notch higher than Washington invariably ended up. He played in thirty-eight games for manager Harry Craft and batted a respectable .293 in 1959.

All told, Herzog managed to last eight years in the majors, wandering from club to club in search of work, and made $18,000 per year in his *best* season—roughly "about what the Cardinals pay our shortstop, Ozzie Smith, every day and a half."[3] To supplement his off-season income, he worked at the only jobs his limited education allowed—as a brick salesman and blue-collar worker for various construction companies, bakeries, and breweries. After a short stretch with Kansas City he variously put on the uniforms of California, Baltimore, and Detroit, before hanging up his spikes in 1963 to become an A's scout. "Whitey Herzog was one of those journeyman players you always heard of but were never sure where," wrote Gary Cartwright, a *Dallas Morning News* reporter who now works for *Texas Monthly* magazine. "You knew he was either a baseball player or the emcee of a kiddies' TV program."

As a ballplayer, Herzog had been smart enough to realize his limitations, and he began to think like a manager, preparing for the day when his career would end even before it had really begun. In the minors, he briefly studied the game under both Casey Stengel and Ralph Houk. In his autobiography, the White Rat considered

Stengel the greatest manager he had ever known, although Houk was "the best at handling people and keeping his players happy."

Herzog scouted for the A's but deplored working for then-Kansas City owner "Charlie O" Finley, who refused to pay a modest $16,000 for a college pitcher named Don Sutton, destined to become a Dodger star. In 1965, he became a Kansas City coach. He enjoyed working with youngsters but could not get along with Finley and quit his $10,000-a-year job. He returned to construction work and had some anxious moments in which he second-guessed his decision to quit until a phone call came from the New York Mets in 1966 offering him a coaching position.

In 1967, Mets general manager Bing Devine promoted Herzog to be his special assistant and later that year named him director of player development. Slowly but surely, Herzog paid his baseball dues, working his way one rung at a time up the baseball ladder. "Two years after I took the job, the Mets won the World Series [1969], and we did it with young players whom I had rushed through the system," said Herzog. "I was probably the best player development man who ever drew a breath."[4]

Herzog toiled seven years with the Mets. He wanted to become a big-league manager but only if he received the right offer from the right organization. He turned down two offers from Finley to manage and one from the hapless Cleveland Indians, knowing that he'd be fired before management would give him the opportunity to turn the franchises around. But when Gil Hodges died of a heart attack, his Mets overlooked him for the managerial opening, and he jumped at the chance to manage the 1973 Texas Rangers, a 54–108 club under Ted Williams the previous year. "When I make a mistake, it's a dandy," wrote the White Rat in his autobiography. He had leaped at the wrong job and was fired on September 8 that same year with a woeful 47–91 mark. Herzog then moved to

California as a third base coach under Dick Williams, a friend and mentor.

In July of 1975, Herzog received a second chance, taking over the Kansas City Royals from the deposed Jack McKeon. All of the moves he had learned from Stengel, Houk, and Dick Williams paid off. He replaced aging outfielder Vada Pinson with Al Cowens and Cookie Rojas with Frank White. The club jelled and finished second. Sportswriters in Kansas City began calling the manager a genius, and when the Royals went on to win Western Division pennants from 1976 to 1978, so did writers across the country. But when the Royals slipped to second in 1979, the club handed an unbelieving Herzog his pink slip. "As a manager, you're always sitting on a keg of dynamite," he said philosophically.[5]

But the manager's record spoke for itself, and in mid-season of 1980, he succeeded the fired Ken Boyer as manager of the St. Louis Cardinals. He had found a home. The Cardinal president, August A. Busch, also appointed him general manager, giving him carte blanche to wheel and deal. And after finishing fourth in 1980, he began a thorough housecleaning. "Well, Chief," he told Busch, "you've got a bunch of prima donnas . . . mean people, some sorry human beings. It's the first time I've ever been scared to walk through my own clubhouse. We've got drug problems, we've got ego problems, and we ain't ever going anywhere."[6]

With the owner's blessing, he unloaded the dead wood and the problem children. His mission was to acquire a team that was tailor-made for the vast confines of Busch Stadium. He wanted fast men on the bases and on defense, as well as pitchers who could keep the ball low, knowing that no one ever hit a home run off a ground ball. And especially, he wanted a reliever who could shut down rallies in late innings.

He signed Darrell Porter, a top-notch player from Kansas City, to be the Cards' catcher. He shipped catcher

Terry Kennedy and six others to San Diego for relief ace Rollie Fingers, starter Bob Shirley, and supersub Gene Tenace. Then he traded Ken Reitz and a rising first baseman named Leon Durham to the Cubs for another bull pen ace, Bruce Sutter, because "our record of defeats after the seventh inning was appalling."[7] Before stunned Cardinal fans could recover, he peddled the newly acquired Fingers to Milwaukee along with Ted Simmons and Pete Vukovich, picking up such young prospects as pitcher Dave LaPoint. In one winter Herzog traded thirteen Cards for ten newcomers, shocking the fans, but the manager didn't care; he wanted a winner, not popularity. And sure enough the Cardinals finished second in both halves of the strike-interrupted 1981 season, good enough to win United Press International's awards for both Executive and Manager of the Year.

But this reincarnation of former Cleveland general manager Frank (Trader) Lane still wasn't satisfied. He wheeled and dealed again during the 1981 offseason to shore up the roster with outfielders Lonnie Smith and Willie McGee, both terrors on the base paths, and shortstop Ozzie Smith. He sent controversial shortstop Garry Templeton to San Diego, condemning him as a man who quit in half the games he played. Then he even got rid of himself as general manager, replacing himself with Joe McDonald. "I prefer the action on the field," he said at the time.

All through the 1982 season, Herzog remained the picture of calm in the dugout, his jaw set and his craggy face exuding confidence. Unlike Earl Weaver, who believed in three-run homers as the focal point of his strategy, Herzog had molded an exciting team that acquired runs the old-fashioned way—they earned them one at a time. His Runnin' Redbirds were singles' hitters who stole their way to second and then scored on bloop singles just over an infielder's outstretched glove. Then Herzog turned over the job of protecting a slim lead to his ace reliever,

Bruce Sutter, and expected his crack defensive crew to rob the enemy of hits. He had created the perfect team for Busch Stadium—a team that sportswriter Tom Boswell of the *Washington Post* wisely called "the first truly modern turf team"—a club "greater than the sum of its parts because each new Card complemented the others."[8]

The 1982 team was made in the image and likeness of its manager. They played exciting baseball, and they won, getting their runs one at a time, but getting them all the same. On September 27, 1982, St. Louis became the first major-league team to clinch their division. They had the fewest home runs in the National League, but Keith Hernandez and George Hendrick knew how to drive home runs, getting 94 and 104 respectively. St. Louis went on to win the league championship from Atlanta in three straight games and then defeated the Milwaukee Brewers in a seven-game World Series. Herzog and his so-called "Whitey-ball" had arrived.

"I don't know what 'Whitey-ball' is, unless it's the same kind of inside baseball that John McGraw was winning with eighty years ago," claimed Herzog. "Big parks with artificial surfaces are here to stay, and if you're going to win on them, you'd better be able to do the things we did in 1982. If I have a motto, it's 'Run, boys, run.' "[9]

But Herzog's club turned big-headed, and 1983 proved a disaster. He had three problems to deal with: big egos, drug use on the team, and inferior pitching. Again he cleaned house after the club dropped to fourth in its division, eleven games behind Philadelphia with a dismal 79–83 record. The club's major problem, said Herzog, was Keith Hernandez, who later admitted in a 1985 Pittsburgh trial of a drug dealer that he'd been a cocaine abuser. At that same trial, Lonnie Smith claimed that he'd shared cocaine with pitcher Joaquin Andujar and Hernandez.

Reluctantly but with dead seriousness, Herzog rebuilt his club for the second time. Smith went into rehabilitation. Hernandez went to the Mets. The manager has never regretted his decision to unload Hernandez, even though the first baseman became a star for the world championship Mets in 1986. "I know he never would have been as good for us as he has been with the Mets," said Herzog in his autobiography. "I tried not to pay much attention to what the fans were saying. If I didn't want to be second-guessed, I'd have to get a new job."

The rebuilding Cardinals finished third in 1984, but regained the National League championship in 1985. The so-called experts had consigned St. Louis to the cellar in preseason, but an MVP year for Willie McGee (56 stolen bases, .353 batting average) and sparkling years by newly acquired Jack Clark (22 home runs, 87 runs batted in, a .281 batting average) made fans forget about Hernandez at last. A rookie named Vince Coleman stole 110 bases to awe the National League, and two starters (Andujar and John Tudor) won twenty-one games apiece.

Unfortunately, the Cards lost the so-called I-70 series against the Royals on the basis of a questionable umpire's decision in the sixth game, which gave Kansas City the opportunity to play and win a seventh game. With basically the same team, Herzog's Cards slipped to third place in their division in 1986, but regained first place to go into the 1987 series thanks to the superb relief pitching of stopper Todd Worrell and Jack Clark's awesome bat. That St. Louis lost the series in seven games to Minnesota was no disgrace. During the year, at one time or another, injuries had taken Jack Clark (ankle injury), John Tudor (broken leg), catcher Tony Pena (fractured thumb), pitcher Danny Cox (broken bone in right foot), and rookie pitcher Joe Magrane (elbow injury) out of the lineup.

Herzog wouldn't deny that he had done a masterful job all season. "I don't think I got any smarter," he told *The Sporting News*, "but I will give myself some credit as a juggler. I had to juggle like hell all season."

What's the secret to his success? Well, while some managers build up clubs through trades and others through free-agency selections and building a strong farm system, Herzog relies upon all three. "They're all available to you. Why shouldn't you use them?" he told writer Rick Hummel, adding that a manager's job was to use the right people in the right place.

And although fans pay to see home run hitters in San Francisco and Atlanta knock the ball out of the park, Herzog continues to drive his National League opponents crazy just one run at a time. "We just go about our business, and we're able to just win," St. Louis hitting star Tom Herr told Hummel. "We don't do anything fancy, except we know how to win."

And now that a certain White Rat from New Athens, Illinois, has reached the top of that baseball ladder he's been climbing, don't look for a let-down. He's worked too hard for too long to get complacent. And that's why, after he retires sometime around the year 1995, he'll be enshrined in the Hall of Fame with his one-time mentor, Casey Stengel.

NOTES

CAP ANSON

1. Martin Appel and Burt Goldblatt, *Baseball's Best: The Hall of Fame Gallery* (New York: McGraw-Hill Book Company, 1980), p. 11.
2. Arthur Bartlett, *Baseball and Mr. Spalding* (New York: Farrar, Straus and Young, Inc., p. 1951), p. 75.
3. Ibid., p. 92.
4. Ibid., p. 92.
5. Ibid., p. 132.
6. Ibid., p. 169.

CONNIE MACK

1. Charles B. Cleveland, *The Great Baseball Managers* (New York: Thomas Y. Crowell Company, 1950), p. 29.
2. Donald Honig, *The Man in the Dugout* (Chicago: Follett Publishing Company, 1977), p. 274.
3. Anna Rothe, ed., *Current Biography 1944* (New York: H. W. Wilson, 1944), p. 432.
4. Connie Mack, *Connie Mack's Baseball Book* (New York: Alfred A. Knopf, 1950), p. 34.
5. *Current Biography 1944*, p. 433.
6. Cleveland, p. 37.
7. Christy Mathewson, *Pitching in a Pinch* (New York: Grosset & Dunlap, 1912), p. 190.
8. Harvey Frommer, *Baseball's Greatest Managers* (New York: Franklin Watts, 1985), p. 185.

9. Honig, p. 168.
10. Cleveland, p. 52.
11. Mathewson, p. 142.
12. John J. McGraw, *My Thirty Years in Baseball* (New York: Boni & Liveright, 1923), pp. 196–197.
13. Mathewson, pp. 279–280.
14. Honig, p. 82.
15. Ibid., p. 82.

FRANK CHANCE

1. Unsigned, "Personal Glimpses: A Chance with Chance" in *Literary Digest* (Volume 46, January 11, 1913), p. 107.
2. Martin Appel and Burt Goldblatt, *Baseball's Best: The Hall of Fame Gallery* (New York: McGraw-Hill Book Company, 1980), p. 68.
3. Charles B. Cleveland, *The Great Baseball Managers* (New York: Thomas Y. Crowell Company, 1950), p. 90.
4. Ibid., p. 89.
5. Ibid., p. 89.
6. Lawrence Ritter, *The Glory of Their Times* (New York: The Macmillan Company, 1966), p. 243.

JOHN J. MCGRAW

1. John J. McGraw, *My Thirty Years in Baseball* (New York: Boni and Liveright, 1923), p. 10.
2. Ibid., pp. 11–12.
3. Frank Graham, *McGraw of the Giants: An Informal Biography* (New York: G. P. Putnam's Sons, 1944), p. 122.
4. Christy Mathewson, *Pitching in a Pinch* (New York: Grosset & Dunlap, 1912), p. 257.
5. Harvey Frommer, *Baseball's Greatest Managers* (New York: Franklin Watts, 1985), p. 168.
6. McGraw, pp. 1–2.
7. Frommer, p. 170.
8. McGraw, pp. 169–170.
9. Frommer, p. 171.
10. Arthur Daley, *Inside Baseball: A Half Century of the National Pastime* (New York: Grosset & Dunlap, 1950), p. 117.

MILLER HUGGINS

1. Martin Appel and Burt Goldblatt, *Baseball's Best: The Hall of Fame Gallery* (New York: McGraw-Hill Book Company, 1980), p. 222.
2. Donald Honig, *The Man in the Dugout* (Chicago: Follett Publishing Company, 1977), p. 172.
3. John Mosedale, *The Greatest of All* (New York: Warner, 1975), pp. 241–242.
4. Ibid., p. 56.

5. Honig, pp. 173–174.
6. Charles B. Cleveland, *The Great Baseball Managers* (New York: Thomas Y. Crowell Company, 1950), p. 99.
7. Lawrence S. Ritter, *The Glory of Their Times* (New York: Macmillan, 1966), p. 229.
8. Leo Durocher with Ed Linn, *Nice Guys Finish Last* (New York: Simon and Schuster, 1975), pp. 60–61.
9. Robert Smith, *Babe Ruth's America* (New York: Thomas Y. Crowell Company, 1974), p. 203.

JOE MCCARTHY
1. Joe Williams, "Busher Joe McCarthy" in *The Saturday Evening Post* (Volume 211, April 15, 1939), p. 80.
2. Curt Smith, "Farmer McCarthy Recalls Pennant Crop" in the *Rochester Democrat and Chronicle*, June 17, 1973.
3. Maury Allen, *Where Have You Gone, Joe DiMaggio?* (New York: New American Library, 1976), p. 20.
4. Ibid., p. 81.
5. Williams, p. 78.
6. Charles B. Cleveland, *The Great Baseball Managers* (New York: Thomas Y. Crowell Company, 1950), p. 120.
7. Honig, p. 93.
8. Ibid., pp. 289–290.
9. Ibid., pp. 93–95.

CASEY STENGEL
1. Robert W. Creamer, *Stengel: His Life and Times* (New York: Simon and Schuster, 1984), pp. 29–30.
2. Maury Allen, *You Could Look It Up.* (New York: Times Books, 1979), p. 46.
3. Creamer, p. 41.
4. Martin Appel and Burt Goldblatt, *Baseball's Best: The Hall of Fame Gallery* (New York: McGraw-Hill Book Company, 1980), p. 355.
5. Gilbert Millstein, "Musings of a Dugout Socrates," in *"I Managed Good, But Boy Did They Play Bad."* Edited by Jim Bouton with Neil Offen (Chicago: Playboy Press, 1973), p. 59.
6. Ibid., p. 60.
7. Appel and Goldblatt, p. 356.
8. Charles B. Cleveland, *The Great Baseball Managers* (New York: Thomas Y. Crowell Company, 1950), pp. 237–238.
9. Creamer, p. 223.
10. Frank Graham, Jr., *Casey Stengel: His Half-Century in Baseball* (New York: The John Day Company, 1958), p. 106.
11. Cleveland, pp. 242–243.
12. Ibid., p. 245.
13. Harvey Frommer, *Baseball's Greatest Managers* (New York: Franklin Watts, 1985), p. 221.

14. Millstein, p. 58.
15. Ibid., p. 58.

LEO DUROCHER
1. Leo Durocher with Ed Linn, *Nice Guys Finish Last* (New York: Simon and Schuster, 1975), pp. 45–46.
2. Donald Honig, *The Man in the Dugout* (Chicago: Follett Publishing Company, 1977), p. 58.
3. Durocher with Linn, p. 117.
4. Charles Dexter, "Mr. Brooklyn Goes to Bat" in *Collier's* (Volume 112, September 11, 1943), p. 78.
5. Honig, p. 249.
6. Charles B. Cleveland, *The Great Baseball Managers* (New York: Thomas Y. Crowell Company, 1950), pp. 169–170.
7. Honig, p. 15.
8. Thomas Kiernan, *The Miracle at Coogan's Bluff* (New York: Thomas Y. Crowell Company, 1975), pp. 79–80.

WALT ALSTON
1. Marjorie Dent Candee, ed., *Current Biography* (The H. W. Wilson Company, 1954), p. 20.
2. Walter Alston with Si Burick, *Alston and the Dodgers* (Garden City, New York: Doubleday & Company, Inc., 1966), p. 30.
3. Melvin Durslag, "Manager with a Hair Shirt," in *I Managed Good But Boy Did They Play Bad."* Edited by Jim Bouton with Neil Offen (Chicago: Playboy Press, 1973), p. 149.
4. Alston, pp. 20–21.
5. Donald Honig, *The Man in the Dugout* (Chicago: Follett Publishing Company, 1977), p. 104.
6. John Roseboro with Bill Libby, *Glory Days with the Dodgers and Other Days with Others* (New York: Atheneum, 1978), pp. 223–225.
7. Maury Wills as told to Steve Gardner, *It Pays to Steal* (Englewood Cliffs, NJ: Prentice-Hall, Inc., 1963), pp. 105–106.
8. Honig, p. 105.
9. Ibid., p. 105.
10. Roseboro, p. 225.
11. Steve Garvey with Skip Rozin, *Garvey* (New York: Times Books, 1986), p. 110.
12. Honig, p. 105.

EARL WEAVER
1. Earl Weaver (John Sammis, ed.), *Winning* (New York: William Morrow & Company, 1972), p. 186.
2. Terry Pluto, *The Earl of Baltimore* (Piscataway, New Jersey: New Century Publishers, 1982), p. 4.
3. Pluto, *The Earl of Baltimore*, p. 14.
4. Ibid., p. ix.

5. Earl Weaver with Terry Pluto, *Weaver on Strategy* (New York: Collier Books, 1984), p. 58.
6. Ibid., p. 67.
7. Earl Weaver with Berry Stainback, *It's What You Learn After You Know It All That Counts* (New York: Doubleday & Company, 1982), p. 179.
8. Pluto, *The Earl of Baltimore*, p. 124.
9. Weaver with Pluto, *Weaver on Strategy*, p. 77.
10. Thomas Boswell, *How Life Imitates the World Series* (New York: Penguin Books, 1983), p. 154.
11. Weaver with Pluto, *Weaver on Strategy*, p. 44.
12. Boswell, p. 155.

SPARKY ANDERSON
1. Charles Moritz, ed., *Current Biography Yearbook* (The H. W. Wilson Company, 1977), p. 24.
2. Ken Kelley, *Playboy* (June 1985), p. 70.
3. Ritter Collett, *The Cincinnati Reds* (The Jordan-Powers Corporation, 1976), p. 165.
4. Moritz, p. 25.
5. Kelley, p. 70.
6. Ibid., p. 75.
7. Ibid., p. 70.

WHITEY HERZOG
1. Whitey Herzog and Kevin Horrigan, *White Rat: A Life in Baseball* (New York: Harper & Row, 1987), p. 29.
2. Ibid., p. 32.
3. Ibid., p. 64.
4. Ibid., p. 79.
5. Harvey Frommer, *Baseball's Greatest Managers* (New York: Franklin Watts, 1985), p. 92.
6. Herzog, p. 117.
7. Frommer, p. 94.
8. Thomas Boswell, *Why Time Begins on Opening Day* (New York: Penguin Books, 1984), pp. 73–74.
9. Herzog, p. 145.

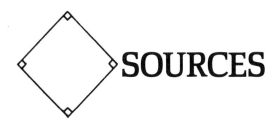

SOURCES

Allen, Maury. *Now Wait a Minute, Casey.* Garden City, New York: Doubleday & Company, 1965.

_____ . *You Could Look It Up.* New York: Times Books, 1979.

_____ . *Where Have You Gone, Joe DiMaggio?* New York: New American Library, 1976.

Allen, Mel, with Frank Graham, Jr. *It Takes Heart.* New York: Harper & Brothers, 1959.

Alston, Walt, with Si Burick. *Alston and the Dodgers.* Garden City, New York: Doubleday & Company, 1966.

Anderson, Sparky, and Si Burick. *The Main Spark.* Garden City, New York: Doubleday & Company, 1978.

Anderson, Sparky, with Dan Ewald. *Bless You Boys.* Chicago: Contemporary Books, 1984.

Appel, Martin, and Burt Goldblatt. *Baseball's Best: The Hall of Fame Gallery.* New York: McGraw-Hill Book Company, 1980.

Bartlett, Arthur. *Baseball and Mr. Spalding.* New York: Farrar, Straus and Young, Inc., 1951.

Berkow, Ira. *Red: A Biography of Red Smith.* New York: Times Books, 1986.

Boswell, Thomas. *How Life Imitates the World Series.* New York: Penguin Books, 1983.

Boswell, Thomas. *Why Time Begins on Opening Day.* New York: Penguin Books, 1984.

Bouton, Jim, with Neil Offen. *"I Managed Good, But Boy Did They Play Bad."* Chicago: Playboy Books, 1973.

Clark, Tom. *The World of Damon Runyon*. New York: Harper & Row, 1978.

Cleveland, Charles B. *The Great Baseball Managers*. New York: Thomas Y. Crowell Company, 1950.

Collett, Ritter. *The Cincinnati Reds*. Virginia Beach, Virginia: The Jordan-Powers Corporation, 1976.

Craig, Roger, with Vern Plagenhoef. *Inside Pitch: Roger Craig's '84 Tiger Journal*. Grand Rapids, Michigan: Wm. B. Eerdmans Publishing Company, 1984.

Creamer, Robert W. *Babe*. New York: Penguin Books, 1983.

——————. *Stengel: His Life and Times*. New York: Simon and Schuster, 1984.

Daley, Arthur. *Inside Baseball: A Half Century of the National Pastime*. New York: Grosset & Dunlap, 1950.

Dexter, Charles, "Mr. Brooklyn Goes to Bat." *Collier's* (September 11, 1943).

Durocher, Leo, with Ed Linn. *Nice Guys Finish Last*. New York: Simon and Schuster, 1975.

Einstein, Charles. *Willie's Time*. New York: J. P. Lippincott Company, 1979.

Fimrite, Ron, "When Will the Bubble Burst?" *Sports Illustrated* (June 11, 1984).

Frommer, Harvey. *Baseball's Greatest Managers*. New York: Franklin Watts, 1985.

Gage, Tom, "Motor City Madmen," *The Sporting News* (April 30, 1984).

Garvey, Steve, with Skip Rozin. *Garvey*. New York: Times Books, 1986.

Graham, Frank, Jr. *Casey Stengel: His Half-Century in Baseball*. New York: The John Day Company, 1958.

Graham, Frank. *McGraw of the Giants*. New York: G. P. Putnam's Sons, 1944.

Herzog, Whitey, and Kevin Horrigan. *White Rat: A Life in Baseball*. New York: Harper & Row, 1987.

Honig, Donald. *The Man in the Dugout*. Chicago: Follett Publishing Company, 1977.

Kahn, Roger. *A Season in the Sun*. New York: Berkley Publishing Company, 1977.

Kahn, Roger. *How the Weather Was*. New York: New American Library, 1973.

Kelley, Ken, "Playboy Interview: Sparky Anderson," *Playboy* (June, 1985).

Kiernan, Thomas. *The Miracle at Coogan's Bluff*. New York: Thomas Y. Crowell Company, 1975.

Luciano, Ron, and David Fisher. *The Umpire Strikes Back*. New York: Bantam Books, 1982.

Mack, Connie. *Connie Mack's Baseball Book*. New York: Alfred A. Knopf, 1950.

Mathewson, Christy. *Pitching in a Pinch*. New York: Grosset & Dunlap, 1912.

McGraw, John J. *My Thirty Years in Baseball*. New York: Boni and Liveright, 1923.

Moore, Jack B. *Joe DiMaggio: A Bio-Bibliography*. New York: Greenwood Press, 1986.

Mosedale, John. *The Greatest of All*. New York: Warner Paperback Library, 1975.

Neft, David S., and Richard M. Cohen, eds. *The Sports Encyclopedia: Baseball*. New York: St. Martin's Press, 1987.

Okrent, Daniel, and Harris Lewine, eds. *The Ultimate Baseball Book*. Boston: Houghton Mifflin Company, 1984.

Pluto, Terry. *The Earl of Baltimore*. Piscataway, NJ: New Century Publishers, 1982.

Pope, Edwin. *Baseball's Greatest Managers*. Garden City, New York: Doubleday & Company, 1960.

Rice, Grantland. *The Tumult and the Shouting*. New York: A. S. Barnes & Company, 1954.

Ritter, Lawrence S. *The Glory of Their Times*. New York: The Macmillan Company, 1966.

Roseboro, John, with Bill Libby. *Glory Days with the Dodgers and Other Days with Others*. New York: Atheneum, 1978.

Rosenthal, Harold. *Baseball's Best Managers*. New York: Bartholomew House, 1961.

Rothe, Anna, ed. *Current Biography*. New York: H. W. Wilson, 1944.

Schaaf, Barbara C. *Mr. Dooley's Chicago*. Garden City, New York: Anchor Press/Doubleday, 1977.

Smith, Curt. "Farmer McCarthy Recalls Pennant Crop." *Rochester Democrat and Chronicle* (June 17, 1973).

Smith, Curt. *Voices of the Game*. South Bend, Indiana: Diamond Communications, 1987.

Smith, Ken. *Baseball's Hall of Fame*. New York: Grosset & Dunlap, 1970.

Smith, Red. *To Absent Friends*. New York: New American Library, 1983.

Smith, Robert. *Babe Ruth's America*. New York: Thomas Y. Crowell Company, 1974.

Sobol, Ken. *Babe Ruth & the American Dream*. New York: Ballantine Books, 1974.

Stengel, Casey, and Harry T. Paxton. *Casey at the Bat*. New York: Random House, 1962.

Thorn, John. *A Century of Baseball Lore*. New York: Hart Publishing Company, Inc., 1974.

Thorn, John. *The National Pastime*. New York: Warner Books, 1987.

Tygiel, Jules. *Baseball's Great Experiment*. New York: Oxford University Press, 1983.

Unsigned, "Personal Glimpses: A Chance with Chance." *Literary Digest* (January 11, 1913).

Veeck, Bill, with Ed Linn. *Veeck—As in Wreck.* New York: Bantam Books, 1962.

Ward, Arch. *The Greatest Sports Stories from the Chicago Tribune.* New York: A. S. Barnes and Company, 1953.

Weaver, Earl, with Terry Pluto. *Weaver on Strategy.* New York: Collier Books, 1984.

Weaver, Earl (John Sammis, ed.). *Winning.* New York: William Morrow & Company, 1972.

Weaver, Earl, with Barry Stainback. *It's What You Learn After You Know It All That Counts.* New York: A Fireside Book/Simon and Schuster, 1982.

Williams, Joe, "Busher Joe McCarthy." *The Saturday Evening Post* (April 15, 1939).

Wills, Maury, as told to Steve Gardner. *It Pays to Steal.* Englewood Cliffs, NJ: Prentice-Hall, Inc., 1963.

Yardley, Jonathan. *Ring: A Biography of Ring Lardner.* New York: Random House, 1977.

INDEX

Aaron, Hank, 115
Adams, Babe, 52
Alexander, Grover Cleveland, 76
Alston, Walt, 105, 106–15
Altobelli, Joe, 125
Amoros, Sandy, 110–11
Anderson, Sparky, 126–34
Andujar, Joaquin, 141, 142
Anson, Cap, 14–23, 26, 37
Archer, Jimmy, 41, 42
Ashburn, Richie, 95
Atlanta Braves, 141
Autry, Gene, 132

Baker, Frank "Home Run," 32, 33, 44
Baltimore Orioles, 11, 48–49, 116–17, 119–25, 129
Bamberger, George, 123
Bancroft, Dave, 53
Barnie, Billy, 48
Barrow, Ed, 63
Barry, Jack, 32, 33
Base stealing, 20, 21, 32, 40, 50–51

Bauer, Hank, 91, 94, 119
Bavasi, Buzzie, 107, 111
Baylor, Don, 41
Bench, Johnny, 129–30
Bender, Chief, 33
Berra, Yogi, 91, 93, 110
"Big inning" concept, 50, 64
Black players, 22–23
Blair, Paul, 120
Boston Braves, 32–33, 88, 89–90
Boston Red Sox, 45, 60, 81–82, 86, 130, 131
Boyer, Ken, 139
Bragan, Bobby, 101
Bremigan, Nick, 122
Bridwell, Al, 42
Bristol, Dave, 129
Britton, Helene, 58, 59
Brooklyn Dodgers, 86, 88, 89, 90, 92–93, 98–103, 104, 107, 109–11
Brown, Bobby, 91
Brown, "Three Finger," 40, 44, 50
Burns, Tommy, 37, 38

Burright, Larry, 113
Busch, August A., 139
Bush, Joe, 87

Campanella, Roy, 110, 111
Casey, Hugh, 102
Cey, Ron, 115
Chance, Frank, 36–45
Chandler, Happy, 101–2
Chicago Cubs, 31–32, 33–34,
    36, 37–45, 76–77, 105, 106
Chicago White Sox, 40, 112
Chicago White Stockings, 14,
    16–22
Cincinnati Reds, 11–12, 58, 98,
    100, 123, 124, 126, 128–32
Clark, Jack, 142
Clarke, Fred, 29
Clarkson, John, 22
Clemente, Roberto, 129
Cleveland Indians, 61, 82, 94,
    104, 122–23, 138
Coakley, Andy, 30
Cobb, Ty, 24–25, 32, 48, 97, 113
Cochrane, Mickey, 34, 99
Coleman, Jerry, 91
Coleman, Vince, 142
College-educated players, 29, 51
Collins, Eddie, 32, 33, 44
Collins, Rip, 109
Combs, Earl, 63, 64
Concepcion, Dave, 129
Corcoran, Larry, 19
Cowens, Al, 139
Cox, Danny, 142
Craft, Harry, 137
Cramer, Roger, 77
Cronin, Joe, 99
Cuellar, Mike, 120, 121
Cutoff play from the outfield, 53

Dalton, Harry, 119
Dark, Alvin, 103
Dauer, Rich, 122
Dean, Dizzy, 98
Dedeaux, Rod, 127
Detroit Tigers, 32, 40, 44, 98,
    99, 126, 132–34

Devine, Bing, 138
DiMaggio, Joe, 78, 81, 91, 92,
    93
Donahue, Tim, 38
Donovan, Wild Bill, 59
Dressen, Chuck, 13, 109, 111,
    113, 128
Driver, William, 85, 86
Drysdale, Don, 111
Dugan, Joe, 63
Duren, Ryne, 92
Durham, Leon, 140
Durocher, Leo, 65, 96–105,
    112–13
Dykes, Jimmy, 25, 31, 80

Earnshaw, George, 33
Eastwick, Rawly, 133
Ehmke, Howard, 33–34
Elliot, Ray, 117
Evans, Jim, 122
Evers, Johnny, 41, 43

Fingers, Rollie, 140
Finley, "Charlie O," 138
Fletcher, Arthur, 65
Ford, Russell, 50
Ford, Whitey, 89, 93
Foster, George, 130
Foxx, Jimmie, 34
Frisch, Frankie, 47, 98
Furillo, Carl, 111

Galehouse, Denny, 82
Garcia, Rick, 122
Garvey, Steve, 114, 115
Gehrig, Lou, 57, 62, 63, 64, 78,
    81, 82–83
Gilliam, Jim "Junior," 110, 111,
    113
Goldsmith, Fred, 19, 20
Goodwin, Jimmy, 117
Gordon, Joe, 79
Gordon, Sid, 103
Gore, George, 21
Grimes, Burleigh, 51, 98
Grove, Lefty, 33, 34, 78

Haas, Mule, 77
Haller, Bill, 123
Harkness, Tim, 113
Harris, Bucky, 13, 90, 105
Hart, James, 22
Hartnett, Gabby, 99
Hauser, Joe, 65
Hendrick, George, 141
Henrich, Tommy, 91, 92
Herman, Billy, 100
Hernandez, Keith, 141, 142
Hernandez, Willie, 133
Herr, Tom, 143
Herzog, Whitey, 135–43
Hit-and-run tactics, 20, 48, 49
Hodges, Gil, 110, 112, 113, 138
Hodges, Russ, 104
Hofman, Artie, 41, 43
Hofman, Bobby, 117
Holmes, Tommy, 126
Hornsby, Rogers, 47, 59
Houk, Ralph, 137, 138
Houston Astros, 105
Howard, Frank, 109
Howsam, Bob, 129
Howser, Dick, 13
Hoyt, Waite, 57, 61, 65
Huggins, Miller, 25, 57–66, 97–98
Hulbert, William, 16, 18
Huston, Tillinghast, 59–60, 61

Jennings, Hughie, 13, 48, 52
Johnson, Speed, 38
Jones, James C., 59
Jones, Sam, 64

Kahn, Roger, 110
Kansas City Athletics, 138
Kansas City Royals, 132, 139, 142
Kaye, Danny, 105
Keeler, Willie, 48, 49
Keller, Charlie, 79–80, 91
Kelley, Joe, 58
Kelly, George "Highpockets," 52–53
Kelly, Mike "King," 20, 21

Kennedy, Terry, 140
Kenney, Albert, 48
Kling, Johnny, 31, 38, 44
Koenig, Mark, 62, 63
Koufax, Sandy, 112, 114–15
Kroh, Kid, 43

Landis, Kenesaw Mountain, 63
Lange, Bill, 37
LaPoint, Dave, 140
Lasorda, Tom, 110
Lavender, Jimmy, 44–45
Lazzeri, Tony, 63, 79
Leach, Tommy, 43
Lindell, Johnny, 91
Lindstrom, Freddy, 52
Lopes, Davey, 115
Lopez, Aurelio, 133
Los Angeles Dodgers, 107, 111–15
Lowenstein, John, 124
Luciano, Ron, 122

McCarthy, Joe, 12, 34, 61, 73–83
McDermott, George, 23
McDonald, Joe, 140
McGee, Willie, 140, 142
McGinnity, Iron Man, 43, 44, 51
McGraw, John Joseph, 28, 32, 39, 46–56, 76, 87, 88
McInnis, Stuffy, 32
Mack, Connie, 24–35, 44, 62, 74, 76
McKeon, Jack, 139
McNally, Dave, 120
MacPhail, Larry, 81, 99, 102
McPhee, Bid, 58
McRae, Hal, 129
Maglie, Sal, 103
Magrane, Joe, 142
Mantle, Mickey, 93
Maranville, Rabbit, 97
Marshall, Mike, 113, 115
Martin, Billy, 13
Martin, Pepper, 98
Mathewson, Christy, 31–32, 44, 47, 50

Mauch, Gene, 12, 13
Mauch, Gus, 91
May, Lee, 130
Mays, Carl, 61
Mays, Willie, 103–4
Mazeroski, Bill, 94
Medwick, Joe, 98
Merkle, Fred, 43
Metro, Charlie, 24
Meusel, Bob, 61, 63, 87
Meusel, Irish, 88
Milwaukee Braves, 110
Milwaukee Brewers, 125, 141
Minnesota Twins, 133, 142
Mize, Johnny, 103, 109
Moon, Wally, 112
Morgan, Joe, 130, 131
Morris, Jack, 133
Murphy, Charles Webb, 40, 44, 45
Murray, Red, 52
Musial, Stan "The Man," 101

Nehf, Art, 54
Newcombe, Don, 104, 110
New York Giants, 22–23, 30, 32, 39, 42–43, 44, 46–47, 50–55, 76, 87–88, 102–5
New York Mets, 94–95, 121, 138, 142
New York Yankees, 11, 12, 45, 52, 53, 57, 59–66, 73–74, 75, 78–81, 87, 90–94, 97–98, 110–11, 131, 136
Nichols, Charles "Kid," 85–86
Norris, Jim, 122–23

Oakland Athletics, 11
O'Doul, Lefty, 45
Ott, Mel, 47, 54–55, 102, 103

Page, Joe, 81, 92, 93
Palmer, Jim, 117, 120
Parrish, Lance, 133
Paul, Gabe, 116–17
Pena, Tony, 142
Perez, Tony, 129, 130

Pesky, Johnny, 135
Pfiester, Jack, 40, 44
Philadelphia Athletics, 15, 24–25, 28–35, 44, 77, 78
Philadephia Phillies, 87, 93, 128
Phoebus, Tom, 120
Pickoff play, 90
Pinson, Vada, 139
Pipgras, George, 64
Pitching rotation, 120–21
Pittsburgh Pirates, 43, 52–53, 63–64, 86–87, 88, 94, 123, 129
Plank, Eddie, 29, 32, 33
Platooning players, 94, 113–14, 120
Podres, Johnny, 110
Porter, Darrell, 139
Powell, Boog, 120
Providence Grays, 19, 21
Pulliam, Henry Clay, 43

Raschi, Vic, 92
Reese, Pee Wee, 100, 110, 111
Reiser, Pete, 100, 101
Reitz, Ken, 140
Relief pitchers, 19, 34, 92, 123, 132–33
Reulbach, Ed, 40
Reynolds, Allie, 92, 93
Rhodes, Dusty, 105
Rickey, Branch, 59, 109
Rickey, Frank, 108
Rizzuto, Phil, 91
Robinson, Brooks, 120
Robinson, Frank, 120
Robinson, Jackie, 92, 110, 111
Robinson, Wilbert, 13, 48, 60, 86
Rojas, Cookie, 139
Rolfe, Red, 79
Root, Charlie, 33
Rose, Pete, 11–12, 123, 124, 129, 130, 131
Roseboro, Johnny, 112, 113, 114
Ruffing, Red, 73, 79
Runyan, Damon, 87

Ruppert, Col. Jacob, 59–60, 63
Russell, Bill, 115
Ruth, Babe, 50, 53–54, 57, 60–61, 63, 64, 66, 81, 86, 97, 98

St. Louis Browns, 22
St. Louis Cardinals, 34, 47, 49, 58–59, 98, 101, 106, 108–9, 118, 139–43
San Diego Padres, 128, 132
San Francisco Giants, 114
Scouting reports, 28–29
Selee, Frank, 38
Shawkey, Bob, 25, 30, 61–62, 63
Shirley, Bob, 140
Sievers, Roy, 117
Simmons, Al, 28, 34
Simmons, Ted, 140
Smith, Lonnie, 140, 141–42
Smith, Ozzie, 140
Snider, Duke, 92, 110, 112
Southworth, Billy, 118
Spahn, Warren, 90, 103
Spalding, Albert, 15, 16–17, 18, 19, 21
Speaker, Tris, 51
Spencer, Daryl, 113
Spitball pitchers, 50
Springstead, Marty, 122, 123
Spring training, 20
Stanky, Eddie, 102, 103, 104
Start, Joe, 18, 19
Steinbrenner, George, 132
Steinfeldt, Harry, 39
Stengel, Casey, 12, 84–95, 111, 114, 120, 137–38
Stengel, Grant, 84
Stoneham, Charles, 47
Stoneham, Horace, 105
Stovey, George, 23
Strang, Sammy, 47
Sunday, Billy, 20, 22
Sutter, Bruce, 140, 141
Sutton, Don, 138

Taft, Charles, 40, 44
Templeton, Garry, 140

Tenace, Gene, 140
Terry, Billy, 55
Texas Rangers, 11, 138
Thomson, Bobby, 104
Tinker, Joe, 42
Topping, Dan, 81, 90
Tudor, John, 142

Umpires, 26, 49, 121–23

Veach, Bobby, 63
Vukovich, John, 130
Vukovich, Pete, 140

Waddell, Rube, 29–30
Wagner, Dick, 131
Wagner, Honus, 44–45, 51
Wagner, Rod, 37
Walberg, Rube, 33
Walker, Moses Fleetwood, 23
Walker, Welday, 23
Walls, Lee, 113
Warneke, Lonnie, 106
Washington Senators, 11, 52, 55, 99, 137
Weaver, Earl, 11, 14, 116–25, 129
Webb, Del, 81
Weisler, Bobby, 117
Weiss, George, 90, 91
Whitaker, Lou, 132
White, Frank, 139
"Whitey-ball," 141
Williams, Dick, 13, 139
Williams, Harry, 54
Williams, Ted, 81–82, 138
Williamson, Ed, 20
Wills, Maury, 112, 113
Wilson, Hack, 34, 76
Witt, Whitey, 87
Woodling, Gene, 91, 94
Worrell, Todd, 142
Wright, George, 19, 21
Wrigley, William, 76

Young, Cy, 29

 # ABOUT THE
AUTHOR

Hank Nuwer, author of *Strategies of the Great Football Coaches* (Watts, 1988) and a contributing writer for *Inside Sports*, also teaches sportswriting at Ball State University in Muncie, Indiana. His work has appeared in such nationally known publications as *The Saturday Evening Post, Outside, GQ, Satellite Orbit*, and *Boston*. He once played first base for a Montreal Expos' farm club to fulfill a magazine assignment.